The Making of the Two Dakotas

The Making of the Two Dakotas

Helen Graham Rezatto

©Copyright by Helen G. Rezatto, 1989.
All rights reserved. First Edition. Published 1989.
Printed in the United States of America.

92 91 90 89   4 3 2 1

Library of Congress #89-061624
ISBN 0-939644-58-4

MEDIA PUBLISHING
(Div. of M.P.M., Inc.)
2440 'O' Street, Suite 202
Lincoln, Nebraska 68510-1125

Dedication

To the memory of my parents
Frederick J. Graham and Ina Randall Graham
and
To the memory of my grandparents
Benjamin and Helen Graham
Marcellus and Minnie Randall
and
To the memory of my favorite aunt—Ava Randall

PIONEERS IN DAKOTA TERRITORY

Family of Marcellus and Minnie Randall. author's mother is the tallest girl in middle of back row. Favorite aunt is on right end with bow in her hair. Ellendale, North Dakota

Property of Helen Rezatto

Table of Contents

AUTHOR'S NOTE

When I was a young girl growing up in Ellendale, North Dakota, I didn't realize that I lived in an obscure country town on the Great Plains which most Americans thought was the end of nowhere. I felt that my universe revolved around me and that getting a good soaking rain was an exhilarating event because then my twin brothers, my oldest brother and myself were allowed to go barefoot to celebrate. Even my taciturn lawyer father smiled when it rained.

I grew up in a big house where my talkative mother's favorite subjects were history, geography, and "the good old days" which sounded bad. Too late, I wish I had listened more attentively to her tales of her big family and the living upstairs above her father's store. She kept scrapbooks about Lewis and Clark, Teddy Roosevelt, James W. Foley, North Dakota's Poet Laureate, and anything related to Dakota. Both grandmothers died fairly young, possibly because they had been over-worked pioneers. Grandpa Graham lived to be old and related colorful stories about life on his homestead near Whitestone Battlefield where General Sully and the Sioux Indians had a big battle.

Grandpa Randall had a beard, and he cussed and spit tobacco into a brass spitoon in his store. He had been a Senator in the First Legislature in 1889. He arrived in Dakota in 1882 in a covered wagon with his wife, two little girls, and my mother, the new baby. Three more girls and one boy eventually joined the family so he never had much chance to talk. Both grandfathers planted many trees to decorate the prairies.

Recently, I was amazed to learn about an unusual subject. Not five miles from my town is the state line along which every half mile is one of 720 quartzite markers forming the boundary between the Two Dakotas. In 1989 I read about these unusual markers in the "Centennial Sentinel." The next time I visit my hometown, I am going to find one of the 720 pillars which have been there for a century on the seventh parallel. And I didn't even know it.

The twins, as President Benjamin Harrison nicknamed North and South Dakota when he signed the statehood proclamations, never have become well-acquainted. In Dakota Territory the distances were too vast. When the railroads finally arrived, they ran east and west, not north and south. Politically, there wasn't much the siblings agreed upon before or after their official simultaneous birth except being Republican and eventually deciding on division and statehood.

The biggest fight the Dakotas ever had was when Yankton lost the territorial capital to Bismarck. Is it possible that we descendants of the pioneers who suffered through wild political brawls still subconsciously react with the same prejudices and emotions our grandparents and great grandparents felt years ago, regardless of which side they were on?

I certainly don't know all the answers. Naturally, I have had to depend upon the writings and research of early historians; some apparently believe the quotation: "History is only a confused heap of facts." How to make honest sense out of it all is a never ending challenge, especially when it is difficult to find two authorities who agree on anything.

For example: Take notable Yankton Chief Strike-the-Ree. Reputable sources can't decide which year he was born, whether or not he was baptized by Captain Meriwether Lewis, what his correct name actually was, how to spell one of his Indian names or one of his white names, or how old he was when he died. My policy is not to choose sides. Let the reader make the difficult decisions.

Doing research on this book, despite many subjects bristling with contradictions was more fun than work: snooping in the library stacks, copying speeches and taking notes, interviewing old timers; reading historical markers, and riding in a speed boat on the Missouri River at Bismarck without hitting a snag or sand bar.

The Two Dakotas have too much fascinating history for one book. I would like to have written more about everyday pioneer life based on firsthand accounts. Perhaps I would like to have tried living in a sod shanty — for a few days. Or living on an early Indian reservation — for one day. I emphasized the Yankton Cession and Greenwood Reservation because my goal was to bring about a better understanding of the inevitable conflicts between the two races. And the Yankton Cession was significant. I wish there had been space to mention more villages and cities and historic places and remarkable people.

Dakota, as we know, means friends or allies. Surely friendship can exist between one-hundred-year-old sisters as well as cooperation can grow between two mature races. A new century is coming up when we can improve the quality of life in the Dakotas under our spacious skies. We can use the pioneers for inspiration.

Helen Graham Rezatto
Rapid City, South Dakota
June, 1989

ACKNOWLEDGMENTS

Both the South Dakota Committee on the Humanities and the North Dakota Council on the Humanities, Affiliates of the National Endowment for the Humanities, provided generous research grants for my project, *The Making of the Two Dakotas*. Both organizations also contributed financial support to enable me to purchase centennial photographs for the completed book. Thank you, the Humanities of the Two Dakotas.

I wish to thank all the members of Western Women in the Arts for sponsoring me.

I am indebted to many people who contributed historical information, encouragement and expertise. Heading the list are John Whalen, Executive Director of the South Dakota Committee on the Humanities, and Everett Albers, Executive Director of the North Dakota Humanities. Dr. George Early, Dr. William Bogard and Dr. Sid Goss were all helpful and genuine Humanities Scholars. Versatile author and rancher Linda Hasselstrom is in a special class by herself, so special thanks to her. Gordon F. Graham, Martin and Kathy Antonen Busch each contributed his and her editorial talents, time and thoughtful advice.

Others who helped in a variety of ways are Virginia Driving Hawk Sneve, Barbara VanNorman, Mary Ethel Francis, JoAnne Messerli, Connie Sarver, Bob Lee, Dr. H.E. Fromm, John Artichoker, Robert F. Karolevitz, J. Randall Graham, Bette Spillers, Wilma Keller, Wayne and Irene Hill, Linfred Schuttler, Earl Chace, James Aplan, Dr. Allen and Rosemary Hill, John W. and Linda Crabtree, Dee Stuart, Ken Norgaard, David Strain, Lorna Sand, Donald D. Dahl, Dorothy Shane, Patricia Bratnober, Gertrude Lampe.

Thanks also to the staffs of these libraries, museums, and other organizations for their cooperation: Bonnie Gardner, Laura Glum, John Borst, and Ann Jenks at the South Dakota Historical Resource Center, Pierre, SD: Forrest Daniel, Jim Davis, Todd Strand, James Sperry and Virginia Heidenreich at the North Dakota Heritage Center, Bismarck, ND: Jean Diggins, Reference Librarian and her staff at the Rapid City Public Library: Bruce Mehlhaff, Lois Affholder, Annabel Dunfee, Mary Margaret Forrette, Linda Long, Darlyne Purpur; Mary Ann Baker, archivist at Devereaux Library, SD School of Mines & Technology, Rapid City, SD; Connie Holltorf and her staff at the Yankton Public Library, Yankton, SD.

Donald J. Binder, Curator at the Yankton County Museum; Marjorie Pontius, librarian at the Case Library for Western Historical Studies, Black Hills State University, Spearfish, SD. Professor John Duff, Joyce Bjork, and Mary Ann Thornburg were most accommodating at the SD School of Mines & Technology Alumni Office and located unusual photographs. Robert Preszler, Curator of the Minnelusa Pioneer Museum, Rapid City, SD. Of course, I still receive countless benefits from reviewing research on the Black Hills used for my first two books from these libraries and museums.

As always, I am happy to express my appreciation to my husband John L. Rezatto for his unbelievable assistance for doing most of the driving and waiting on my research trips. The last time I thanked him in print for his supporting me through a big project, I prophesied that he was well on his way to becoming a gourmet cook. Now he has reached that pinnacle. And he continues to be a sensible, astute and diplomatic first reader. Thank you again, John.

Short quotations from the following copyrighted works are used by permission of the publishers or the author or both:

Dakota Territory 1861-1889, by Howard R. Lamar, Yale University Press, 1966.

History Of North Dakota by Elwyn B. Robinson, University Of Nebraska Press, 1966.

History Of South Dakota, third edition, by Herbert S. Schell, University of Nebraska Press, 1975.

Over A Century Of Leadership; South Dakota Territorial And State Governors, 1861-1987 — A Retrospective. Edited and revised by Lynwood E. Oyos. Sioux Falls, SD: Center for Western Studies, Augustana College, 1987.

Lessons From Chouteau Creek: Yankton Memories Of Territorial Intrigue. by Renee Sansom-Flood. Sioux Falls, SD: Center for Western Studies, Augustana College, 1986.

"Sitting Bull: The Image of a 'Great Man,' " by Herbert T. Hoover, in *The Last Years Of Sitting Bull.* Bismarck, North Dakota Heritage Center, State Historical Society of North Dakota, 1984.

Challenge The South Dakota Story by Robert F. Karolevitz, Brevet Press, Inc. Sioux Falls, SD, 1975.

Brevet's South Dakota Historical Markers, Jane Hunt, Ed. Brevet Press, Sioux Falls, SD, 1975.

Boots And Saddles or Life in Dakota with General Custer, by Elizabeth B. Custer. Copyright © 1961 by the University of Oklahoma Press.

Following The Guidon, by Elizabeth B. Custer. New edition Copyright © 1966 by the University of Oklahoma Press.

PART ONE

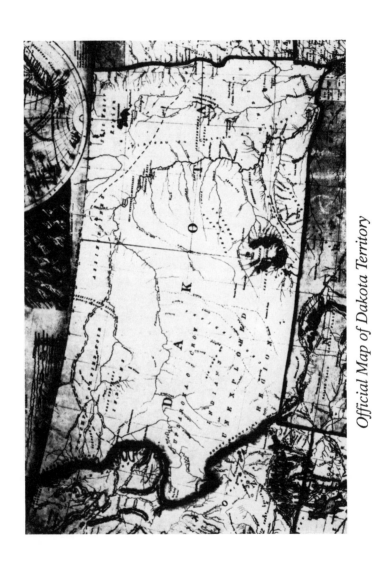

Official Map of Dakota Territory

From the picture collection of the State Historical Society of North Dakota.

THE MAKING OF THE TWO DAKOTAS

Dakota — Where's That?

In the early 19th century, probably no one in the thirteen original states plus Vermont, Kentucky, and Tennessee had ever heard the word "Dakota" as the name of a specific place. Perhaps some had heard of the Dakota or Sioux Indians who were reputed to be the most fierce and war-like of any Indian tribes in that vast, unknown frontier out west.

There is no record of when Dakota became a loosely-used designation to identify a boundless, unorganized region out there somewhere. Perhaps Dakota was up by the North Pole.

Dakota, even though it did not yet have that name, was an unorganized territory of the New World where land ownership had changed frequently because of political intrigue, secret treaties, and often disputed claims based on explorations by powerful European countries. The flags of Spain, England, and France had all flown over portions of Dakota at one time or another.

Thomas Jefferson and his Big Dream

The entire region was acquired from France and called Louisiana Territory, which included most of Dakota. Thomas Jefferson, who became President of the United States in 1801, was the visionary who was determined to know more about it.

His most cherished dream came true when the young nation under his leadership was at last able to acquire all of Louisiana, an undefended and massive territory. It included all the watershed of the Mississippi River from the Gulf of Mexico to Canada, and from the Rocky Mountains to the Mississippi River. The entire region was greater in size than the United States of that day.

Thomas Jefferson

From the picture collection of the State Historical Society of North Dakota.

Jefferson got the best bargain in American history. Napoleon of France sold the huge land tract to the United States for a mere fifteen million dollars, about four cents an acre. Our canny third President was not only a brilliant negotiator; he was also a scholar and a scientist fired by an adventurous spirit.

Jefferson chose Captain Meriwether Lewis and Captain William Clark to lead the exploration into the wilderness of the Louisiana Purchase, to take the scientific expedition up the Missouri River to its source, to cross the Rocky Mountains, and then to find the Columbia River which was believed to lead directly to the Pacific Ocean.

Not even Jefferson knew how high or wide the Rockies were or how treacherous and long the Missouri was. It was at that time thought to be the main thoroughfare to the Pacific and reputed to be the "orneriest river that God ever made."

Lewis and Clark Expedition Leaves St. Louis for the Pacific Ocean

At last, in May 1804, Lewis and Clark with their forty-five carefully selected men boarded a long keelboat and two smaller pirogues which could either be sailed or rowed. They left St.

Captain Meriwether Lewis

From the picture collection of the State Historical Society of North Dakota.

Louis, heading up the Missouri River toward the Pacific Ocean. With specific instructions from President Jefferson, they were to open up a river route for fur trade and other commerce. They were also to study the Indian tribes, their languages and customs, to make friends with them and avoid hostilities, and to inform the native Americans through interpreters that they now belonged to the Great White Father back in Washington.

Captain William Clark

From the picture collection of the State Historical Society of North Dakota.

Jefferson instructed Lewis and Clark to keep accurate journals describing all the birds, animals, plants, rivers, geology, weather — everything of interest. Then when they reached the Pacific, they were to claim the Oregon Territory for the United States: a challenging order.

The small flotilla soon found themselves battling the Missouri (called Smoky Water by the Indians and Big Muddy by the whites), a swift-flowing but deceptively shallow river. The crew struggled to avoid the shifting sand bars, snags, careening logs hurtling down on them, and sawyers which were hidden trees embedded in the river bottom that could rip out the bottoms of their boats. They fought whirlpools to avoid being swung dangerously close to the constant cave-ins of the river banks.

These strong young men, taking turns using oars, poles, and towlines, managed to move their boats upstream barely fifteen miles a day in the changeable channel with its treacherous currents. Yes, the Missouri lived up to its ugly reputation and deserved every curse flung at it.

The crew, when not navigating or watching for Indians, found time to admire the changing scenery of the forests along the shores and the rolling plains beyond. A hunter shot the first buffalo where the Missouri begins to angle west near present-day Vermillion. They dined very well on juicy buffalo meat. They often saw endless herds blackening the prairie as far as the eye could see and giant grizzlies lumbering along the shore. They also ate elk, deer, wild turkey, Missouri catfish, and drank the muddy water after giving it time to settle.

Visit with the Yankton Sioux

The first Indians they visited were the friendly Yankton Sioux. Here they fortunately met a good interpreter named Pierre Dorion, a white fur trader who had married a Yankton Sioux and had lived in the area for over twenty years. Most historians believe Dorion was the first white man to settle permanently in southern Dakota. Dorion suggested to the captains that they set the prairie on fire to announce their arrival and to signal their willingness to council.

The Yanktons were cordial and served them dog meat, which Lewis found delicious and Clark disliked. Through interpreters they exchanged speeches with the Yanktons, applauded the Indian dances while rewarding the hospitality with gifts selected from their twenty-three bales of Indian presents: knives, tobacco, bells, needles, medals, fish hooks, beads, calico ruffled shirts.

Doane Robinson,
first SD State Historian

From the picture collection of the State
Historical Society of South Dakota.

Although the following incident is not mentioned in the Lewis and Clark Journals, the story is told by the first South Dakota Historian, Doane Robinson, who vouched for its accuracy: A new-born male child born in the Yankton Sioux camp was brought proudly to show the explorers. Ceremoniously, Captain Lewis wrapped the child in the Stars and Stripes as a gesture of friendship and good will and prophesied that the babe would become a great leader and a true friend to the white race.

This baby grew up to become the notable Chief Strike-the- Ree, and as he matured, he was often told of how the white explorers had baptized him as an American citizen. The tradition of his naturalization became the proudest heritage of Strike-the-Ree or Struck-by-the-Ree, popularly known as "Old Strike."

Lewis and Clark Have Tense Visit with the Teton Sioux

Lewis and Clark next visited the Teton Sioux, who were encamped near present-day Pierre. The Yanktons had warned the captains that the Tetons were aggressive and dangerous, that they constantly forced other tribes farther north, and had intimidated Spanish and French traders.

The expedition's experience with the Tetons was their first test and show-down with hostile Indians. The Tetons grabbed the two ropes of the pirogues, insisted that the boats could go no farther, and aimed their bows and arrows at the white men.

Coolly, Lewis ordered the men to pick up their rifles and to aim the large swivel cannon on the keel boat at the Indians lined up on the shore. After more blustering and threatening behavior on both sides, the Tetons decided to adopt the friendly host role. They invited the whites to a feast and a scalp dance where sixty-five scalps were displayed as well as at least fifty Indian prisoners. At night several important chiefs insisted on sleeping on the keelboat. Despite heavy guards, the two captains and their men had little sleep. At last the four-day ordeal ended, and the men gladly took on the Missouri River again as their foe. They named the island where they had anchored "Bad-Humored Island."

Lewis and Clark Visit with Arikara Agriculturists

Their next encounter with Indians went very smoothly. They stopped at an Arikara or Ree village at the mouth of the Grand River in what is now north central South Dakota near Mobridge. The Arikaras lived in dome-shaped earth lodges and cultivated large fields of squash, corn, beans, tobacco, and melons which lured other tribes to come and trade. Captain Clark was amazed that the Arikaras refused the whiskey he offered them. Because the tribe had much contact with white traders, the entire village was infected with venereal disease. However, the men had a pleasant time and rested from their stressful visit with the Tetons whom they knew continually attacked the Arikaras and tried to force them northward.

The center of attention was York, the huge black servant of Captain Clark. The Indians had never seen a black man before; they examined him from head to toe and tried to rub the black off his skin. York was a showman, and through an interpreter told his audience that he had been a wild animal before his master caught and tamed him. Making horrible faces and roaring like an animal, York made the children run away screaming. He responded to the promiscuous Indian women and was always a great favorite with both sexes of the Indian tribes they met. Clark was afraid York sometimes got carried away and recorded in his journal with his inimitable spelling: "York made himself more turribal than we wished him to doe."

Wintering with the Mandan Indians and Finding Sakakawea

After fifty-four days in what is now South Dakota, the expedition headed straight north up the Missouri into northern Dakota. Winter was coming and the weather was getting frosty toward the end of October. Lewis and Clark were thankful to arrive at the Mandan villages about sixty miles north of present-day Bismarck near the junction of the Knife and Missouri Rivers where they planned to spend the winter.

Several Indian tribes, including the Hidatsas, the Mandans, and the Arikaras lived peacefully together in a settlement of about 4500, probably the largest Indian concentration on the Missouri River and in the Midwest.

Like the Arikaras, the Mandans were agriculturalists and raised a variety of crops in addition to hunting buffalo and other game and catching fish. Their lodges were similar to the style of the Arikaras with large, dome-shaped earth roofs and room for several families inside.

For their winter quarters, Lewis and Clark chose a location a few miles from the five Indian villages. The men began building a triangular-shaped structure which they named Fort Mandan. Soon the American flag flew over the western-most outpost of the United States.

Here they had the good fortune to acquire for a guide a sixteen-year-old pregnant Shoshoni Indian girl named Sakakawea, the Bird Woman. She had been captured by the Hidatsas in the foothills of the Rockies, treated as a slave, and then married a half-breed named Charbonneau who won her as a prize in a gambling game.

Lewis and Clark had met the couple when they hired Charbonneau as an interpreter who persuaded them that his young wife could be a guide — which they doubted. As it turned out, her talents and character were far superior to those of her husband.

The men spent a cold but pleasant winter at Fort Mandan where they enjoyed the camaraderie with the friendly Mandans with whom they traded axes and scrapers made by their blacksmiths in exchange for corn. During the long winter nights the men told tall tales by the fireplace. When the fiddler played, the men sang lustily and danced clogs and reels with each other. On holidays they celebrated with drinking and feasting.

When spring came, the men prepared for the next phase of their exploration into unknown country. Sakakawea strapped her baby Baptiste (nicknamed Pompey) onto a papoose board on her back and carried him all the way to the Pacific. The group left Fort Mandan on April 7, 1805, prepared for the many perils ahead. Because the Mandans had previously ventured into the Rocky Mountain region, they were able to provide helpful information about the terrain and the river courses, even making portable maps on animal skins for the explorers.

Sakakawea proved herself to be loyal and courageous. When the instruments and valuable equipment sometimes ended up in the river, she was the one who quickly rescued them. She collected herbs and roots that were edible and medicinal. Her greatest contribution was her reliable recollection of how to reach the Shoshoni tribe from whom she had been separated since she was twelve years old. The appearance of a woman and a baby accompanying the expedition reassured suspicious Indian observers along the way that this was not a war party, thus reinforcing the message of the American flags the boats always flew.

Sakakawea

Statue on Capitol

Grounds

Bismark, ND

From the picture collection
of theS tate Historical
Society of North Dakota

In what is now western Montana, and after the men had managed the difficult portage around the Great Falls of the Missouri, Sakakawea began recognizing familiar landmarks. She told Lewis and Clark (who called her Janey) that the place where the Missouri divided into three branches was close by. She was right, and they soon arrived at the unimpressive source of the Missouri. They named it "Three Forks" and decided to follow the southwest branch they had named in honor of Thomas Jefferson.

Meeting with the Shoshonis and Sakakawea's Brother, the Chief

At last they met the elusive Shoshonis, Sakakawea's tribe, who lived in the high mountains. As Sakakawea began to interpret the exchange of greetings, she suddenly recognized Chief Cameahwait as her brother. She ran to him, threw her blanket over his head, and clasped him in her arms, crying. He responded affectionately. It was an emotional reunion and one whose dramatic effect was electrifying for the spectators. However, the most practical result of this reunion was that it eased the way for the Shoshonis to help Lewis and Clark.

Crossing the Continental Divide in Winter

The chief and his people agreed to sell scarce horses to the expedition, who knew their boats were useless in the turbulent, cascading mountain rivers. Sakakawea's brother gave them good advice on the best way to cross the Continental Divide on horseback and provided them with guides over the Nez Perce trail. They also met another friendly tribe, the Flatheads, who shared their food and pointed the way west.

The dense forests and snow-covered peaks of the Northern Rockies were almost impassable. Trails were slippery, and the horses kept falling and even sliding into canyons. The weather was miserable with snow and sleet, and there was no game. Starving and exhausted, the group, including Sakakawea with the baby strapped to her back, killed and divided up the meat: one, two, then three colts, a coyote, and a raven.

At the end of the rugged Lolo Trail over the Bitteroot mountains, they met the accommodating Nez Perces who drew a map on a white elk skin to show them where they were and where they were going. Chief Twisted Hair volunteered to guide them in canoes to the Snake River and thence to the Columbia with its swift rushing water.

Reaching the Pacific at Last

On November 8, 1805, despite their exhaustion, cold, and hunger, they were overwhelmed with excitement to see the Pacific Ocean they had dreamed about as it emerged out of the clammy mists. The expedition spent a hard winter on the cold, rainy Oregon coast near present day Astoria, Oregon. They built Fort Clatsop, which was always rain-soaked. Decent food, kind Indians, and warmth were scarce. To pass the time the men, instructed by Sakakawea, made 359 pairs of moccasins, while Lewis and Clark worked over their notes on Indians, weather, plants and animals, and organized the stacks of information into readable form.

Homeward-bound Trail

In March the party was glad to leave the noisy, damp shores of the Pacific for home, going down the same waterways and land trails they had followed on their way up. Occasionally the expedition divided into two groups to enable them to explore more territory. Sakakawea again demonstrated her ability to guide by leading the Clark contingent over the Bozeman Pass and eventually to the Yellowstone River. Lewis took the Missouri route and stopped to retrieve caches of boats and supplies they had hidden almost two years before.

The rendezvous point for the two groups was at the junction of the Yellowstone River where its yellowish water brightened the muddy Missouri near present-day Williston, ND. The reunion was spoiled because they were attacked by clouds of mosquitoes which covered the sun. It was impossible to talk without inhaling them into the mouth and nose. Little Pompey suffered greatly.

Again, though the entire expedition was at the mercy of the Missouri River, going downstream was much easier than going up. The canoes often made from forty to seventy miles a day. They soon arrived at the Mandan villages where they were welcomed by their old friends the Mandans. Following Jefferson's wishes that the captains should bring back some Indians, the two were able to persuade Chief

Sheheke and his wife of the Mandans, and interpreter Rene Jessaume, his wife and two children, to accompany the expedition back to white civilization for a visit.

Sadly they said farewell to the Mandans and to Sakakawea, Pompey and Charbonneau, who was paid $500.33 1/3. Sakakawea was the only member of the expedition who received no payment.

Overnight Stop with the Arikaras

In southern Dakota they stopped overnight at the Arikara village near present-day Mobridge where they had stayed on the upward journey. About 350 Cheyenne warriors were also visitors. The captains held a council with the chiefs of both tribes and, as was their custom, orated about keeping peace between tribes. They invited chiefs from both tribes to accompany them to Washington but the Indians declined. The Cheyennes asked them questions about trapping beaver and selling the pelts. Obviously news about the growing fur trade was increasing.

The voyageurs raced happily down the Missouri which on an especially good day seemed almost like an old friend. They met several groups of fur traders going up river who wanted to hear about their travels.

St. Louis at Last

Two years and four months from the time the expedition had left St. Louis, they reached the awesome turbulence where the Missouri meets the Mississippi. It was only a few miles farther to St. Louis. The captains and the crew were all dressed in buckskins. The proud leaders watched their men salute smartly, fire three rounds with their blunderbusses, and wield their oars with great showmanship. They enjoyed the scene greatly as the canoes pulled into the levee.

The news had preceded them. An excited crowd of whites, blacks, and Indians made a colorful picture with their contrasting skin tones and bright costumes. They pushed and jostled to get a look at the miraculous explorers. Only God knew where they had been and what they had seen. But here they were, returned from the dead, and the crowd cheered until they were hoarse while the cannons roared a deafening welcome. September 23, 1806, was a never-to-be-forgotten day in St. Louis.

Captain Lewis immediately sent off to President Jefferson by fastest mail the thrilling message of their safe return. Then the two captains with their Indian friends made another long trip by horseback to Washington, D.C. At the capital city they were all greeted by an elated President Jefferson. The entire group was entertained in the White House, honored and praised and celebrated. Congress voted double pay and land grants for each member of the expedition (including York) except Sakakawea, who received an honorary certificate she could not read.

Accomplishments Surpass Disappointments

The explorers had not accomplished everything they had set out to do: they had not discovered the fabled Northwest Passage. They had not found the easiest or the shortest or the most practical route for commerce to reach the Pacific. Actually, their route was one of the most difficult.

Nevertheless the expedition's accomplishments and successes were magnificent. They were the first white men to travel up the Missouri to its source, to cross the Continental Divide on horseback in winter, and to maneuver canoes through the Snake and Columbia Rivers to the Pacific Ocean. They were often famished and exhausted in body and spirit, but they had kept going.

By the time they returned to St. Louis, they had covered 7,689 miles by boats, on horseback, and on foot. Only one life had been lost. On the upward trip Sergeant Floyd was assumed to have died of a ruptured appendix.

The captains had brought back priceless detailed and accurate information about an unknown region. They had carefully recorded scientific data with hundreds of descriptions and many accurate drawings of birds, animals, plants, and trees. Captain Clark, a skilled cartographer, had laboriously made invaluable maps.

Their surveys and presence in Oregon Territory helped strengthen America's claim to the Oregon country (not part of the Louisiana Purchase).

Best of all, they made friends with numerous Indian tribes and had only two hostile encounters which they had handled with coolness and restraint. The two white captains recognized the worth and dignity of the Indians and demonstrated respect for their religion and culture. To maintain peace between whites and Indians as well as between Indian tribes had been their conscientious objective.

Effects of the Expedition

The two brave young captains, both Virginia natives, led the way West. Their successful journey fired the imagination of the American people. It inspired thousands of fur traders to take their boats up a variety of waterways and encouraged immigrants in covered wagons to pioneer the Oregon Trail and other routes farther south.

Thirteen states were eventually created from the Louisiana Purchase, including North and South Dakota in 1889.

No, Lewis and Clark were not the first white men to explore the Missouri River valley in the Dakotas, but they earned more firsts than any other explorers to visit the region. Both North Dakota and South Dakota have a special right to claim these genuine heroes for their own.

Because of Lewis and Clark, America would never be the same again — and neither would Dakota.

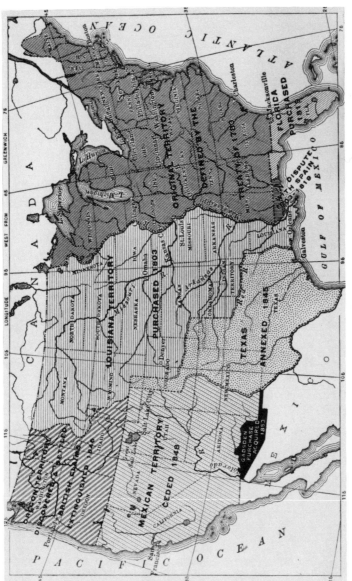

Map of the United States defining the Louisiana Purchase

From the picture collection of the State Historical Society of North Dakota

PART TWO

THE MAKING OF THE TWO DAKOTAS

Explorers and Events
Before and After Lewis and Clark

La Verendrye visits the Mandans in Northern Dakota

Pierre La Verendrye and two of his sons visited both northern and southern Dakota over sixty years before Lewis and Clark started on their epic journey to the Pacific. The Verendryes are credited with being the first white men to visit Dakota. Verendrye, a French-Canadian from Montreal, came by canoe down Lake Superior to the border waters of Canada and the present United States. He was searching for a river through the western mountains to the fabled River of the West, long a favorite pursuit of explorers in North America, hoping to find a short cut to the western sea. To finance Verendrye's explorations, the French King had promised him a monopoly on the fur trade.

Verendrye and his sons built a line of small forts in Canada and eventually journeyed southwest to the Dakota prairies about whose Indians they had heard many colorful tales. The rumor was that a tribe of Indians called the Mandans could tell them how to achieve their quest and what lay west of the mighty river.

The Mandans, who seemed destined to become favorite Indians of

many explorers, greeted
Verendrye and his group like old
friends. They carried La
Verendrye on a buffalo robe into
their settlement of 130 lodges,
begged him to stay in that particular village, and promised they
would become like his children.

This Canadian explorer kept
the earliest written record of
northern Dakota Indians on the
Upper Missouri; it was an excellent diary packed with details.
He was amazed at the many
varieties of food that his hosts
served him for one meal: corn,
wheat, beans, pumpkins, squash,
sunflowers, tobacco — even sugar
from the sap of a box elder tree.

Pierre La Verendrye

Photograph courtesy of the State
Historical Society of South Dakota

"Interior of Mandan Earth Lodge" painting by Karl Bodmer

From the picture collection of the State Historical Society of North Dakota

Of course, buffalo and Missouri river fish were the Mandans' principal meat.

Verendrye also admired the Mandan earth lodges with many divided into apartments. He noted how the earthen roofs were reinforced with branches and grass. Protecting the villages were medieval-like fortifications including a fort, deep ditches or moats, and a palisade.

At that time the Mandan earth lodges faced the center of the village where there was a large wooden structure meant to represent the big canoe of the first man. The Mandans believed they were the First Man; the First Man built a mammoth canoe, and during a flood he crowded his people into it. The big canoe and its human cargo floated on the high water and came to rest on top of a hill overlooking the Cannonball River in northern Dakota.

Mystifying to scholars is Verendrye's description of the white physical characteristics of some of the Mandans. In his diary Verendrye described Mandans with light skins, fair hair, and even blue eyes. These unusual physical differences were also mentioned by Lewis and Clark, artist George Catlin, and Prince Maximilian of Wied, all guests at various times in the hospitable Mandan villages. A few scholars, including Catlin, believed that the Mandans had descended from a Welsh colony who had visited them at an unknown date. The origin of the Mandans has never been determined to everyone's satisfaction.

Although the Mandans were knowledgeable people, they did not know any short route to the western sea. However, by the time Lewis and Clark arrived, they had collected considerable information about the Rocky Mountain region. They related entertaining legends around the campfire, including the canoe saving the people from a flood—a common myth among the religions of the world, Christian and non-Christian.

Verendrye, after a stimulating ten-day visit with the Mandans, gave his hosts a lead plate claiming the land for the French king. Although this act was recorded in his diary, this first lead plate was never found.

Verendrye became very sick and left the village to slog through December snows many miles back to his tiny Canadian fort. He never again visited Dakota but his sons carried on his explorations.

Verendrye Brothers Explore Southern Dakota

In April, 1742, Verendrye sent his sons, Francois and Louis Verendrye, on another search for feasible routes to the western sea. The journals of the Verendrye brothers were not as detailed or well-written as their father's diary, but historians believe that they had seen the Big Horn Mountains from a distance but probably did not travel far beyond the Black Hills in western Dakota. Some historians speculate that the brothers may have climbed Bear Butte, the historic laccolith, as did so many other historic personages who came after them, including Crazy Horse and Custer.

In 1913 a group of children were playing on a bluff overlooking Fort Pierre and the Missouri River when they noticed a strange crusted object sticking out of the ground. Excited, the children showed their foreign-looking discovery to their parents who presented it to local historians who knew the lead plate was mentioned in the Verendrye journal.

Yes, it was the second Verendrye lead plate that Francois and Louis Verendrye had buried there 170 years earlier. On both sides of the plate was writing in French and Latin: their names, the date, March 30, 1743; and the arms and inscription of Louis XV, King of France. After the brothers erected a small pyramid of stones over their buried claim for France, they turned northward to visit the Mandan villages again, the most popular haven for travelers on the Missouri River. From there the Verendryes journeyed back to Canada.

This plate is the first record of white men on southern Dakota soil. Today, the lead evidence is displayed in the State Historical Museum at Pierre, South Dakota. After many years of exploration in the western parts of the United States and Canada, La Verendrye did not find that elusive river leading to the western sea. He received little payment or acclaim for his life's work. He died a sad and disillusioned

State Historical Marker locating the place where the Verendryes buried lead tablet claiming the land for France.

Photograph courtesy of the South Dakota State Historical Society

man, this explorer who had ranged through much of western Canada and western America, who had canoed down Lake Superior to the Boundary waters between Canada and the United States, and who had discovered the Red River of the North and the Upper Missouri.

According to historian Elwyn Robinson, no white man arrived in northern Dakota for about half a century after the explorations of the the Verendryes. "But during this time, two things from the whites greatly influenced the Indians of the region: horses, which gave them new freedom and power, and small pox which cut them down." Robinson believes that in 1782 and possibly also 1786, epidemics killed thousands of Indians of the northern plains. Many Mandans and Hidatsas were known to have died. Throughout the 19th century small pox epidemics continued to ravage the Indian tribes, leaving the stench of death and desolation over the prairies.

The Verendryes had many firsts; they were the first white men to visit both northern and southern Dakota. They had been the first white men to make friends with the remarkable Mandan Indians.

No wonder the Verendrye name and the story of their lead plate found at Fort Pierre will live forever in Dakota history.

More than 150 years before the two Dakotas became states, an unknown number of Spaniards, French and English began trapping, trading, and competing with each other for furs in the upper midwest. The fur trade in the northern half of the United States and southern Canada was actually the pioneer industry of the nation. The British dominated the fur trade, and there was great rivalry among all the trading companies and their countries.

Historians believe that French voyageurs had, in all probability, reached the upper end of Lake Superior before the Pilgrims landed at Plymouth Rock in 1620. Paddling in canoes, dugouts, and mackinaws, these adventurers plied the lakes and rivers of north central America in search of the lucrative furs. When their boats were loaded with pelts, they went down the Missouri to St. Louis to make contact with the buyers in Philadelphia, Chicago, New York, and the urban centers of Europe including London and Paris—even as far away as Canton, China.

As the name implies, the fur trade was a business—and a very profitable one for the whites because their offerings to the Indians were so cheaply purchased compared to the stupendous rewards they eventually received for the furs they obtained.

Fur trapping was the chief industry of the United States in the 1830's

From the picture collection of the State Historical Society of North Dakota

Many of the traders did their own trapping, particularly of beaver, the staple of the fur trade. The best way to capture beaver was with the five-pound steel trap, and the hunters became skillful at using this device and often had to wade into icy water to retrieve their victims and reconnoiter the lodges and dams of these coveted animals.

Other trader-trappers worked for the big fur companies like Hudson's Bay. The traders were welcomed with great hospitality by the Indian tribes who could never get enough of the fascinating merchandise these entrepreneurs offered them. Many traders established genuine friendships with the Indians, often took Indian wives, and lived among the natives for months.

The white traders exchanged knives, guns, gunpowder, blankets, salt, sugar, coffee, cooking pots, mirrors, tobacco, and liquor for the harvest of furs the Indians piled in a rich shimmering display. Eventually buffalo robes, bear hides, and deer skins were added to the beaver pelts. Other prized products were bear and buffalo tallow. Casks of dried buffalo tongues were considered a great delicacy by both races.

The number of fur traders who reached Dakota before the Verendryes is unknown. The only proof of French exploration in southern Dakota is the retrieved lead plate the Verendrye brothers had buried in 1743 near Fort Pierre. As has been noted, La Verendrye's journal detailing his visit to the Mandan Indians in northern Dakota has been preserved.

Despite the European and Canadian penetration of the wilderness, it took the dazzling success and wide-spread publicity in 1806 about the safe return of the Lewis and Clark Expedition to stimulate the rapid expansion of the American fur trade.

The conquering heroes, as they may justifiably be called, had rejoined civilization very much alive after ascending and descending the wicked Missouri. It reassured and encouraged others to know Lewis and Clark had survived the Big Muddy, wild Indians, dangerous animals, and starvation; they had crossed the Rocky Mountains in winter to reach the foggy Pacific coast; they had brought back proof of the bounty and resources of the west they. Others decided they could do it all too. Lewis and Clark oepned the west to an enthusiastic nation and revitalized the fur trade.

It was no surprise that the returning boats of the expedition met fur traders in Dakota waters already battling upstream when Lewis and Clark were going downstream to St. Louis just as fast as the swift Missouri current would take them. St. Louis was the magnet that attracted the fur traders from Dakota and all points northwest in the wilderness. Their boats stacked with furs, the boatmen sang the rollicking songs of the French voyageurs as they swished down the big river on their fast return trip to St. Louis, the commercial distribution point for the fur trade.

Manuel Lisa — King of the Missouri

Manuel Lisa, a Spanish-American born in New Orleans, was the first trader to penetrate the far reaches of the Missouri valley. More than any other person, he may be credited with the dominance achieved by the American companies in the competitive fur trade of the Northwest. He was also a prominent figure in assisting the cause of the United States during the War of 1812 with England. He soon became known as the "King of the Missouri."

Although Lisa could not speak English (only Spanish and a little French), he was a

Manuel Lisa

From the picture collection of the State Historical Society of North Dakota

master at dealing with the Indians. He knew when to be conciliatory and when to be severe; he was shrewd and vigorous, an indefatigable leader who invariably worked harder than his assistants.

Lisa made his first trip up the Missouri shortly after the return of Lewis and Clark. He engaged George Drouilliard, a member of the expedition as his partner. Lisa organized the Missouri Fur Company which became highly successful in the Dakota country and brought large quantities of furs down the river for many years.

Pierre Chouteau, Sr., an old rival of Lisa's, joined the company and was authorized to check out the fur traders in the area and renew any licenses of the American citizens. If he found any British traders, Chouteau was to revoke their licenses and order them to return to St. Louis, then to leave the country to avoid arrest. The British traders were unpopular with Americans because they encouraged the Sioux not to trade with Americans but to constantly harass them. The British were reminded that Dakota was a big portion of the Louisiana Purchase, a vast domain belonging to the United States. Trespassers were not wanted.

Lisa's most renowned exploit is also hailed as one of the most legendary events in frontier history, one which was discussed and argued about for years. This accomplishment was Lisa's race up the Missouri to overtake the Hunt expedition managed by Wilson Price Hunt, the partner of John Jacob Astor. Astor had just organized the Pacific Fur Company with plans to concentrate efforts in Oregon.

Although the Hunt party had left St. Louis nineteen days before Lisa, the indomitable Spaniard was determined to overtake them for reasons of safety. The two groups could join forces and present a formidable appearance when their boats passed the villages of the hostile Sioux and Arikara, thus deterring the Indians from attack and from trying to prevent the numerous boats from ascending higher up the Missouri.

Hunt had about a 240-mile head start, and the race stretched over a period of two months. Lisa sent messages by trusted runners requesting that Hunt wait for him with an explanation of the reasons.

Hunt replied that he would wait, but instead he redoubled his efforts to outdistance Lisa. The reason for Hunt's deception was probably due to previous disagreements which had strained relations between the two men.

Hunt's favorable reply spurred on Manuel Lisa. According to several accounts, Lisa, a former sea captain, took command of the tiller himself for hours at a time without rest. He urged his expert keelboatmen to redouble their efforts and encouraged them to sing French voyageur songs to keep up their spirits while navigating the rambunctious river with its dangerous snags and currents.

At last Lisa caught up with the Hunt party at the point where Pierre, South Dakota, is now located, and the two groups camped a short distance from each other. Hunt and Lisa, threatening a duel, began to quarrel so violently that Henry Brackenbridge and another scientist with Lisa prevented the two from trying to kill each other.

Finally the two rival troops ascended the Missouri together with the boats of each leader traveling on opposite sides of the river. There was no communication between them.

At the mouth of the Cheyenne River they were all delayed by a vast herd of buffalo taking their time crossing the Missouri River. At last the fur traders arrived at the Arikara village. By this time the two belligerent leaders had cooled off; they decided to shake hands and the two warring groups entered the village together as friends and allies.

The imposing group had no trouble with the Arikaras. The Hunt party stayed for six weeks at the village before starting off overland with its eighty-two horses acquired from the Arikaras in exchange for guns and ammunition which the Rees wanted to use to fight the Sioux. The route of the Overland Astorians wound west of present-day Mobridge along the Grand River valley on their long and arduous trek to the Pacific Ocean to set up a fur empire.

Lisa went as far up the river as the Mandan villages north of present day Bismarck and returned the 1500 miles to St. Louis in October, 1811. In May, 1812, Lisa plowed up the Big Muddy with two barges and eighty-seven men. In addition to the usual trading goods, the barge carried cows, pigs, cats, and chickens. Thus, Manuel Lisa brought the first domestic cattle into Dakota where they have existed ever since.

This time the group spent the winter at abandoned Fort Mandan built by Lewis and Clark. To pass the time, Lisa may have read and reread his favorite book *Don Quixote*.

Even after the War of 1812 with England began, Lisa continued his fur trade, being one of the few who did. In 1814 General William Clark, the Captain Clark of the noted expedition whom the Indians called Chief Red Head, was then in charge of Indian territories. Recognizing Lisa's ability to control the Indians, Clark appointed him as subagent for all the Indian tribes on the upper Missouri, hoping his Latin diplomacy would keep the Missouri Indians neutral.

While performing his duties, Lisa spent much time boating up and down the big highway he knew so well, counseling tribes on their behavior, securing promises of loyalty to the United States, and organizing the Indian parties to harass the allies of the English, the Santee Sioux from Minnesota and the Yanktonais.

During the war he also spent considerable time building forts on the Missouri River. He built Fort Manuel, his headquarters, just below the 46th parallel, the present-day boundary between the Dakotas. It included a blacksmith shop, a warehouse, large living quarters — all surrounded by a stockade.

Fort Manuel was destroyed by fire a year later and fifteen whites were killed, reportedly by a group of hostile Sioux incited by the British Northwest Company. For this reason Doane Robinson, South Dakota State Historian, said the burning of Fort Manuel was a clear link between South Dakota and the War of 1812.

Other forts mentioned included Fort Lisa near Omaha, an unnamed fort on the island between Chamberlain and Pierre, and one on the Big Bend.

At the Big Bend fort Lisa raised horned cattle, hogs, and chickens. He supplied seeds and instructed the Indians in raising vegetables for the fort which he operated as a refuge for ancient and ailing Indians. About 65 people, white and Indian, lived at the fort.

Historian Robinson summarized Lisa's influence: "Within our section was domiciled a master mind whose wise strategy was of great significance. But for it the boundary dividing American and British dominance in America might have been far different from what it now is."

In 1817 when Lisa resigned his commission as subagent, he wrote a celebrated letter of resignation to General Clark, defending himself from charges his rivals made that he cheated both the government and the Indians. (One wonders how his letter was communicated; if written in Spanish, could General Clark or linguists on his staff translate it? Or did Manuel Lisa have an accomplished secretary who translated his Spanish into English? When Lisa traveled, did an interpreter always accompany him?)

Here are excerpts from Lisa's long letter of resignation:

First, I put into my operation great activity. I go a great distance while some are considering whether they will start today or tomorrow.... Cheat the Indians! The respect and friendship which they have for me, the security of my possessions in the heart of their country respond to this charge, and declare with voices louder than the tongues of men that it cannot be true.... I appear as a benefactor and not a pillager of Indians.

After peace was declared, Lisa persuaded forty chiefs of the Missouri River tribes under his jurisdiction to descend the Missouri to attend a council involving treaties of peace and friendship with the United States.

Lisa had three wives, including two at one time, a beautiful Indian girl named Mitain and a white girl who had been an Indian prisoner. He had a number of children with both wives. His third wife was a charming widow named Mary Keeney, a devout Presbyterian, beloved by all who knew her, including Manuel, a Catholic. As a bride, the third Senora Lisa accompanied her husband on a trip up the river and is regarded as the first white woman to ascend the Upper Missouri.

During the twelve years of fur trading, Lisa made at least twelve round trips up and down the water highway. Chittenden, the historian of the fur era, estimated that "he must have spent the equivalent of three solid years battling the Missouri and could not have traveled less than 26,000 miles by river.... Of the twelve winters, he probably spent nearly eight in the wilderness."

Lisa apparently had a charismatic personality which dominated others in his life-long striving to become wealthy from the fur trade. During his successful career he achieved wealth, fame, and a reputation for fair dealing and benevolence in his relationship with Indians. On Lisa's final trip in 1820, he returned to St. Louis in apparent good health, then became ill of an unknown disease, and died suddenly at age 48. His death was a contrast to his vigorous life because "he slipped away into the great unknown without distressing struggles."

In her laudatory biography, Kathryn French concludes the story of his life with these lines: "To the pioneer of the west all honor is due for his courage and endurance, but to the vanguard of the pioneer, Manual Lisa, the west and the nation owe a tribute of love and esteem."

Fur Trading Posts and Military Forts

At the height of the fur trade from 1807 to about 1845, many fur trading posts were established; some were merely small log cabins near an Indian village where a salaried agent presided. Usually there was a large stockade enclosing a court where trading was done, and often a cannon pointed at the gate to intimidate the Indians. As the years passed and the needs of the Dakota frontier changed, forts often overlapped in their purposes and combined their services. There were fur trading forts, military forts for the protection of the settlers and the railroads and later, forts where annuities were doled out to reservation Indians.

Along the Missouri in northern Dakota the trading post of Fort Berthold, just east of what is now the Montana line, also known as Like-a-Fishook Village, was begun by the Mandan and Gros Ventre

Fort Rice

From the picture collection of the State Historical Society of North Dakota

tribes. Fort Rice was built as a base of supplies for General Alfred Sully who had trouble catching up with the Sioux long enough to fight a battle. Fort Abraham Lincoln was the post built to protect the building of the railroads and became the home of Custer's renowned Seventh Cavalry. Fort Yates and Fort Totten were built as reservation posts. There were many other forts too which came and went like Fort Atkinson and Fort Stevenson.

Fort Abercrombie on the lower Red River withstood a long siege during the Sioux Uprising in Minnesota in 1862. It was used in early pioneer days as a rendezvous for the emigrant trains struggling westward to the Montana gold fields.

Fort Union, the pride of the Missouri River

Of all the forts in the northwest, the best known was Fort Union, built by the American Fur Company. It was an imposing structure overlooking the junction of the Missouri and Yellowstone Rivers. Ruled by Scotsman Kenneth McKenzie, the notorious "King of the

Kenneth McKenzie

*From the picture collection of the State
Historical Society of North Dakota*

Upper Missouri," this fur emporium resembled a medieval castle and was an impregnable fortress against the Indians and the wilderness.

Many travelers who have stopped at Fort Union have described the scene as their boats approached this outpost of civilization. It was situated high on a bluff with a huge American flag flying over the fort on a 65-foot pole. The cannons boomed a welcome, and the musketry for the boat fired a response. Passengers descended on a gangplank not far from the massive double gates of the fort, which was decorated with a painting depicting a peace treaty being signed by Indians and whites.

It was estimated that at the height of the steamboat era approximately 10,000 people traveled as far as Fort Union simply for the adventure of riding safely in comparative comfort through the wilds with a chance to see real Indians.

Many important and distinguished guests were entertained at Fort Union. In 1832 artist George Catlin was a passenger on the *Yellowstone*, the first steamboat which made it that far up the Missouri. He painted realistic pictures of Indian life and wrote sympathetically about the various tribes he visited. In 1843 Prince Maximilian of Wied stayed two weeks at Fort Union and later wrote a wonderful book, *Travels in the Interior of North America*, which was illustrated by sketches made by artist Karl Bodmer who had accompanied the Prince up the Missouri. James Audubon, an ornithologist and scientist, brought his own taxidermist so he could have birds killed and preserved to serve as models for his later bird paintings.

Four Bears, the famed Mandan chief wearing war bonnet and holding coup stick.
Painting by Karl Bodmer

From the picture collection of the State
Historical Society of North Dakota

When entertaining dignitaries, McKenzie often dressed in colorful gold-braided uniforms or sometimes in a medieval suit of armor. Many lavish banquets were served at his table on linen cloths with fine china and silver.

The awed guests sipped their wine cooled with ice from the ice house as they gazed in wonder around the rooms decorated in regal splendor with art work, glass windows, ornate fireplaces, and oriental rugs. Often the guests were entertained by a quartet playing bagpipes. It was inded a treat to be a guest at Fort Union, actually a well-equipped village within its massive stockade.

Liquor for the Fur Trade

McKenzie became a wealthy man through his illegal trade with the Indians. Although the federal government had laws against "introducing" liquor to the Indians, McKenzie and other traders managed to smuggle it. Chittenden described how the contraband was stored in every conceivable kind of container: short, flat kegs which would rest conveniently on the sides of pack mules; when carried by water, the liquor was concealed in floor barrels and bales of merchandise. After McKenzie was arrested, he built his own still at Fort Mandan and made his own liquor with corn obtained from the Mandan Indians.

At Fort Union, as well as at many other forts, the Indians were hereded into an enclosure, served a few powerful drinks until they were stupefied enough to accept mostly water. Then they willingly turned over their piles of furs to the traders while thirstily holding out their cups for more. When the business transaction was completed, they were locked up—men, women, and often children "until the whole band was utterly vanquished and surrendered body and soul to the incomparable trader," reported Chittenden. After a drunken orgy, lasting two or three days, the Indians had nothing to show for their trading enterprise except head-splitting hangovers.

Pembina Settlement in Northeastern Dakota

In 1797 the Northwestern Fur Company, a French company from Montreal, sent Alexander Henry to the Red River of the North, now the North Dakota-Minnesota boundary, to establish fur posts. He came with four canoes carrying twenty-one people by way of Lake Superior, through the boundary lakes of present-day Minnesota and Canada, and then to the Red River. There were also two horses led along the bank and 45 Indian canoes packed with Chippewa Indians. Henry named the party the "Red River Brigade."

Because of the large number of beaver dams, Henry built his first fort at the present site of Park River, ND; he later built another post at Pembina now on the North Dakota-Canadian border, where the Pembina River joins the Red River. Henry kept a lengthy journal full of fascinating details, including shocking accounts about how the traders demoralized and cheated the Indians by giving them liquor in exchange for furs.

In his journal Henry often callously mentions the fearful problems the liquor used in trade brought the Indians even though he was the original villain of the debacles: "Men and women have been drinking a match for three days and three nights, during which it has been drink, fight, drink—fight—and drink and fight again,—guns, axes, and knives their weapons. Very disagreeable."

Pembina Settlement in 1822

From the picture collection of the State Historical Society of North Dakota

In 1797 Henry established the Pembina fur trading post, the first settlement in what became Dakota Territory. The flagstaff for Fort Pembina was a single oak stick, "seventy-five feet high without splicing" and flew the British flag, a red flag with the crosses of St. George of England and St. Anthony of Scotland.

In 1801, the Hudson's Bay Company and XY Company, two British companies, also established trading posts in the same locations; consequently, the fur companies had many violent disagreements and troubles among themselves. These British posts were established long before there were sod shanties west of the Missouri River and before Lewis and Clark went on their journey.

In 1812, only six years after Lewis and Clark had returned triumphant, the first permanent settlement in northern Dakota was established by Lord Selkirk from Scotland, a philanthropist who was a poor organizer and manager of his plans. Eventually, a Selkirk Colony was also established and later became Winnipeg, Manitoba, in Canada.

Over a period of about three years Lord Selkirk began offering a total of 270 Scottish Highlanders and some Irish—all of whom were paupers because of their landowners—free trips to America and free land when they arrived. The Selkirk Colony members underwent much suffering in reaching their destination by ship and then overland to the middle of the continent. Even after these immigrants were settled in new log cabins at Pembina and treated kindly, their life was hard because of the altercations between Lord Selkirk and the Northwest Fur Company in which many people were killed.

These hardy but experienced Scotsmen and Irish had to adjust to a new life in a strange land, including how to hunt the abundant game.

The Northwestern Company also built a fort which they named Grand Forks at the junction of the Red River and the Red Lake River. These trading posts were the only ones in northeastern Dakota when the Selkirk settlers arrived in 1812.

Throughout the entire Dakota region and beyond, liquor eventually became the most prized medium of exchange from the viewpoint of both Indians and whites. These Native Americans had never tasted intoxicating liquor before, had no immunity to the poison, and it affected them violently; sometimes they even frightened the traders who gave it to them.

The Pembina Buffalo Hunt

A picturesque and exciting scene was always the June Pembina buffalo hunt when many Metis (French-Canadians who had married Chippewas) set off on an extensive hunting expedition. The purpose of these hunts was to go out on the prairies where the lushest feeding grounds of the buffalo were and to bring home enough meat to last for at least a year.

This animated caravan resembled a village in motion: it consisted of hunters on horses and wives and children driving the squeaky Red River carts, pulled by horses or oxen. Families brought huge supplies of food, tents, and equipment for hunting, skinning buffalo, and making pemmican, dried buffalo meat.

Occasionally, the big hunting party traveled hundreds of miles, even as far west as Fort Union, depending on how quickly the hunters located a big herd. The hunters often killed over a thousand buffalo in one day.

The well-organized group was led by a guide bearing a flag. Ten captains were elected to obey the chief, and ten soldiers were responsible to the captain. The council made certain laws including these: "No buffaloes to be run on the Sabbath. No party to fork off, lag behind, or go before without permission.... Every captain in turn, to patrol the camp and keep guard. For the first trespass against these laws the offended to have his saddle and bridle cut up.... Any person convicted of a theft to be brought to the middle of the camp and the crier to call out his or her name three times, adding the word "thief" each time, according to Fish and Black in *A Brief History of North Dakota*.

Red River Cart Train near Canadian Border

From the picture collection of the State Historical Society of North Dakota

In 1820 there were 540 carts assembled for the hunt; in 1840 there were 1630 people and a proportionate number of carts. The total cost of the 1840 trip was estimated at $120,000. The Metis often allowed their neighbors—the Scots, Irish, and English—to join their exciting hunts. The hunts continued until about 1870 when the buffalo had almost disappeared. But the stories of these adventurous expeditions are still told and retold when the varied and mixed descendants of the Pembina pioneers reminisce about their unusual heritage.

Memorable Pembina Pioneers

Jolly Joe Rolette was well-known to all the people living in the Red River Valley, probably even as far as Hudson's Bay where the Red River of the North drains. Rollette received a good education in New York City, but returned to the frontier wearing buckskins and radiating enthusiasm for hard work even though he cared little for money.

Rolette was an industrious fur trader and is credited with starting a line of creaking Red River carts, made completely of wood and drawn by oxen or horses. The carts turned out to be an effective method of transportation and thus diverted much fur traffic from Hudson's Bay Company in Canada to St. Paul. His active business enterprise is credited with helping to make

Joseph Rolette

From the picture collection of the State Historical Society of North Dakota

St. Paul a city. Rolette was elected a member of the Minnesota legislature when the Pembina area was part of Minnesota. According to historian Clement Lounsberry, "the City of St. Paul, Minn. has embalmed Rolette in its history as one of its saviors." Through a political shenanigan, he saved the capital from being removed from St. Paul, and today his portrait hangs in the Minnesota state capitol building.

The British fur companies in Canada were always in competitive conflict with those in the United States. The British could provide plenty of liquor to the Indians which the Americans could not do if they obeyed the law. When the British set up an illegal post on American ground not far from Rolette, he took a dozen half-breeds, burned their warehouses to the ground and drove the frightened invaders back to Canada.

Jolly Joe was the personification of the pioneer spirit and known as the "Kingpin of the Fur Traders." He was the first pioneer to register his homestead claim in his name in northern Dakota in 1868. Rolette County, bordering Canada, is named for him. This first homesteader was buried in an unmarked grave when he died in 1929. Later the Old Settlers Group in the Red River Valley bought him a handsome marker.

Charles Cavalier, a native of a large and important Springfield, Illinois family and a close friend of Abraham Lincoln, became a Pembina pioneer in 1851. Isabella Murray, his future wife came from a prominent family with twelve children. Her father, born in Scotland, was a chief officer of the Hudson's Bay Company, and one of her grandfathers had been an original settler of the Selkirk colony.

In 1856 Charles Cavalier and Isabella Murray were married when she was sixteen. After their wedding in Winnipeg, they came down the Red River against the current in their two dug-out canoes; at Pembina they crossed to the Crow Wing waterway leading to St. Paul, camping every night and fording many streams. In the wilderness they were attacked by mosquitoes, forced to hide from bears and wolves, and encountered 300 Chippewas enroute to fight the Sioux. It took almost a month to reach Fort Ridgley where they were happy to prepare breakfast on their own campfire.

Throughout their adventurous and often arduous life together in the Pembina area, they survived many harsh pioneer experiences—floods, fires, blizzards, grasshoppers, hostile Indians, and hostile white rivals. The Cavaliers had five children.

Both Charles and Isabella enjoyed writing. Colorful accounts of their lives and observations are preserved. Before his marriage, Cavalier was assistant postmaster at Pembina, then postmaster. He wrote a detailed account of the problems of handling the mail when the postage for a letter

Charles Cavalier

From the picture collection of the State Historical Society of North Dakota

was from six cents to 25 cents, depending on the distance. "Go as you please on foot, by horseback, cart, or canoe, anything to get there," was the motto he advised for mail carriers. He explained how the mail from Winnipeg was generally carried by two men in a cart or dog train or on their backs.

Cavalier wrote: "Our carriers were all half breeds, the best and most reliable men to be had. Our best man was called 'Savage' who had the endurance of a blood hound, tough as an oak knot, fearless and faithful." Cavalier, who had been the first state librarian of Minnesota, was a great story teller and people enjoyed listening to his tales and experiences. He was correspondent for the Smithsonian Institute in Washington and sent a Red River cart to the organization.

When Cavalier became a collector of customs for the government, he, his wife, and a clerk were the only English-speaking people in Pembina. The couple were both popular and respected; they contributed greatly to the quality of life in the Red River Valley of

Dakota. Cavalier County on the Canadian border is named for these renowned pioneers.

Explorers Keep Coming to Dakota

Jedediah Smith, who always carried his Bible, was with the General Ashley party trading for horses at the Arikara village near present-day Mobridge, South Dakota, when the Indians launched a surprise attack. There were many dead and wounded, especially among the whites. Smith knelt on the keelboat and asked the Lord's blessings for the souls of the dead. Smith's celebrated prayer in 1823 became known as the first recorded act of Christian worship in what is now South Dakota.

In southern Dakota, in 1823, Smith led about a dozen men walking from Fort Kiowa on the Missouri River near present-day Chamberlain to the Wind River country in Wyoming. On this long trek Jed Smith was attacked by a grizzly bear and lost an ear. It was sewn on by James Clyman. Clyman kept a diary of the trip, but he was vague about many details, including the routes taken.

However, historians have agreed that the Jed Smith party were the first white men to enter the Black Hills, and that they must have passed through the Buffalo Gap break into the sacred Paha Sapa of the Sioux.

Smith was killed in 1831 at age 32 by Comanches while he was scouting on the Santa Fe Trail. However, his record as a trail-blazer and explorer ranks high in the annals of the West. South Dakotans honor him for his immortal prayer after a murderous battle and for his entrance into the Black Hills. Perhaps his most outstanding "first" is that an official national law, enacted in his memory in June, 1832, prohibited intoxicants from being sold in Indian territory.

Among other noted explorers to visit Dakota were Dr. Joseph Nicollet, the French scientist, and John C. Fremont, then a young man who later became known as "The Pathfinder." In 1856, Fremont ran unsuccessfully as the first Republican candidate for the Presidency of the United States. The two explorers came up the Missouri to Fort Pierre where they stayed several weeks preparing for their surveying and mapping expedition.

A few days later a Yankton chief with his daughter and an interpreter came to the fort and offerd the pretty girl as a wife for Nicolett. The older man graciously declined, explaining that he already had a wife and the Great Father disapproved of his having two. "But here," said the clever Frenchman, "is Mr. Fremont who has no wife at all." Embarrassed, Fremont said he was very flattered but he was going far away and would not be coming back. The explorers concluded the incident by presenting handsome gifts to both the chief and his daughter, who seemed well-satisfied.

Equipped with horses, wagons, ammunition, and provisions, the two surveyors with six assistants rode horses out from Fort Pierre to explore the James River, Devils Lake, Lake Traverse, and the Big Sioux River, as well as all unusual geology and geography they found.

On the evening of July 3rd, 1836, a patriotic Fremont clambered to the top of Medicine Knoll near present-day Blunt, South Dakota, where he fired guns and rockets to celebrate Independence Day. The main contributions of Nicolett and Fremont in their several expeditions were the wonderfully accurate maps they made of the Dakota country, unsurpassed for decades.

Steamboating on the Upper Missouri

In 1831, a new invention, the steamboat, steamed up the Missouri from St. Louis to the present site of Pierre, South Dakota. Pierre Chouteau, Jr., who had been a young colleague of Manuel Lisa, was then manager of the western agents of the American Fur Company. He and Kenneth McKenzie, the notorious agent at Fort Union, had been promoting the use of steamboats and defended their practicality, despite many doubts by other river men. These two experts were sure that flat-bottomed steamboats could survive the currents, skim the shallow waters, and avoid the snags on the Missouri.

The first trip of the *Yellowstone* to the Upper Missouri was a great event which revolutionized river traffic. Clumsy keelboats took almost a whole season to make the round trip while a steamer could do it in a few weeks, if lucky.

The *Yellowstone's* destination was old Fort Tecumseh, a rickety fort made of driftwood. Chouteau ordered it rebuilt and moved back from the crumbling shores of the erratic river. The new fort was renamed Fort Pierre Choteau, then shortened to Fort Pierre.

Pierre Chouteau, Jr., agent for the American Fur Company

From the picture collection of the State Historical Society of North Dakota

Fort Pierre was actually a larger fort than Fort Union but not as impressive inside or out, although it was fortified in much the same way. The rebuilt fort had about twenty buildings, two large blockhouses, and a stockade. Traveler T. Culbertston described it as an imposing structure "with a porch along its whole front, windows in the roof, and a bell on top, and above it the old weather cock, looking for all the world like a Dutch tavern." Fort Pierre was always a gratifying sight to travelers approaching it by the river or by land.

In 1832 the *Yellowstone,* which had traveled the 1800 miles from St. Louis to Fort Union and had encountered no problems, had Pierre Chouteau, Jr. as passenge from Fort Pierre for the ascent. The artist George Catlin was also a passenger on this trip, his first visit to the Upper Missouri to paint and study the Indians. Catlin described how frightened the Indians were when the steamboat appeared, firing cannons and blowing whistles at every Indian village. Terrified, the Indians threw themselves on the ground and killed their horses and

Fort Pierre as seen in painting by Swiss artist Karl Bodmer

Photograph courtesy of the State Historical Society of South Dakota

dogs in sacrifice to the Great Spirit to save them from the horrors of
the "Big Thunder Canoe" or the "Fireboat-That-Walks-on-Water."

In addition to freight, steamboats carried many passengers: il-
lustrious artists and writer, scientists, explorers, fur traders, military
men, adventurers, European royalty—a motley group who traveled
the big highway for business, observation, and excitement. Soon the
fleet of steamers made as many as 100 round trips every summer.
There were many wrecks. The Missouri did not change to accom-
modate the steamers; the boats had to adapt to the idiosyncrasies of
the river. To lift their boats over the sand bars, the river men devised
a fantastic and complicated operation called "grasshoppering." Two
long spars, resembling stilts, one on each side of the bow, were set in
the sand. With capstan turning and the paddle-wheel revolving, the
boat was lifted up and pushed forward, resembling the hopping movement of a grasshopper. Steamboats burned from twenty to thirty
cords of wood a day. Early steamboats stopped and men tore down

deserted trading posts and forts for their wood. Later, men called "woodhawks" lived along the wooded banks of the Missouri and cut down trees, mostly cottonwood, to sell to steamboats.

The Missionaries Brought Christianity to the Dakota Frontier

Father Pierre Jean DeSmet was probably the best-known and most respected Catholic priest in America in his day, from 1851 until his death in 1873. Four American presidents—Pierce, Buchanan, Lincoln, and Johnson—asked his advice and requested the services of this Belgian-born Jesuit. He was often present at treaty-signing between the whites and the Indians.

Father Pierre Jean DeSmet, a Belgian-born Jesuit Priest

Photograph courtesy of the State Historical Society of South Dakota

DeSmet traveled thousands of miles on foot, on horseback and by boat throughout the western frontier—converting many Indians to Christianity, nursing them when they had small pox and cholera, and carrying messages from the "Great Father" in Washington to numerous tribes. He underwent many hardships in performing his work. DeSmet was reputed to have more influence with Indians than any other white man. Even Sitting Bull trusted "Black Robe" and invited him to his lodge to speak to the Sioux.

The first Prostestant missionaries in southern and eastern Dakota were Presbyterian ministers, the Reverend Thomas Williamson and the Reverend Stephen Riggs and their wives. The Reverend Riggs in 1840 preached the first sermon in southern Dakota at Fort Pierre to

Indians and whites. Williamson and Riggs translated the Bible and hymn books into the Eastern Dakota language and oreated a Dakota-English dictionary.

In 1818 in the Red River Valley of northern Dakota, two young priests, Joseph Provencher and Severe Dumoulin, came as missionaries to the settlers. In 1845 Father George Belcourt built a mission at Pembina. From 1818 to 1880, thirty-three priests and four bishops worked in the Pembina district. The priests worked with the Indians and the Metis baptizing and performing marriages and burial services. A priest always accompanied the Pembina Hunt.

In general the immigrants to Dakota already represented many churches when they came to America, thus bringing a variety of Christian religions to the frontier. Many pioneer ministers worked hard to bring Christianity to the Indian tribes who worshipped Wakan, the Great Spirit, who had many similarities to the God of the Christian religion. For many years the government tried to stamp out Indian religions.

George Catlin wrote a "Creed" in which he said, in part: "I love a people who keep the commandments without ever having read them or heard them preached from the pulpit." And "I love a people whose religion is all the same, and who are free from religious animosities."

"Missouri River Snags" by Karl Bodmer from Travels in the Interior of North America by Maximilian

From the picture collection of the State Historical Society of North Dakota

PART THREE

THE MAKING OF THE TWO DAKOTAS

The Yankton Cession Opens the Way

The lucrative fur trade grew to be the chief industry of the United States with Dakota an important contributor. About the middle of the nineteenth century it began to decline on the Missouri River and its tributaries, as well as on the Red River of the North and beyond. Two major reasons for this were that the beavers had been over-trapped, and beaver hats were no longer fashionable with Americans and Europeans who had previously bought them by the thousands. Ever since Lewis and Clark had led the way, the fur traders and trappers had extended their territory throughout the Midwest and Northwest, leaving it almost barren of fur-bearing animals. During the best years many traders and large fur companies had become rich — but not the Indians.

The decline of the fur trade was unfortunate for all concerned. But the Indians and the whites with their relentless hunting had brought about the decimation of the seemingly endless herds of buffalo (estimated at about sixty million). The animal products were no longer there in abundance, and the Indians had learned to depend on the fur traders for the guns and ammunition, the knives and the trinkets, the liquor and the tobacco, and other popular trade merchandise. It was a dismal situation for the red men, and the whites lost a flourishing business.

The Dakota Sioux, the Arikara, the Assiniboin, the Chippewa, the Mandan, the Hidatsa, and the Cheyenne could no longer rely on Uncle Buffalo to provide them with food, clothing, tools, and other necessities. The Indians had managed to find a use for almost every part of a buffalo's body: the lining of the paunch served as an effective water bucket, axes and spoons were made from the shoulder blades, glue from the hooves, spoons and ladles from the long horns, even a brush from the short tail. The buffalo was the Indian's supply center, the giver of life, the center of the universe.

Sometimes wasteful whites killed the buffalo just to eat his delicious tongue or for sport or to demonstrate marksmanship, leaving the carcass to rot. Because of the decline of the buffalo population, many Indians went hungry.

Pressures Increasing on the Indians

The Indian tribes of Dakota objected to the increasing number of whites invading their sacred territory, slaughtering the buffalo, and despoiling nature's bounty. The white leaders with their interpreters tried to persuade these native Americans to sell their valuable land, then hoped to restrict them to reservations where they would be content to hunt on the shrinking prairie. The Indians objected to these plans for their future. For centuries the Indians had ranged freely and hunted unmolested in a wilderness domain where herds of buffalo had made the earth tremble, where Indians fought Indians, not whites.

The Confusing Influences of the White World

The influences of the whites created confusion in the Indian world. The white man used mysterious instruments for measuring land and distance and the stars; he presented ambiguous treaties with strange markings and inexplainable words like latitude and longitude and

46th parallel. He kept up insistent proddings to "Just put your mark here," or "Just touch the pen." He made promises of generous annuities for years to come and of other white man benefits like teaching Indians how to plow. The white man had come often with his whiskey for trade, his small pox and cholera epidemics. Often these disasters made the heart of the Indian turn bad.

Manifest Destiny Takes Over

The United States government and its citizens believed they had an inalienable right to take over the immense expanse Jefferson had acquired with the Louisiana Purchase, despite the fact that countless Indian tribes had lived there for ages. The government mulled over plans on how to manage and restrict, and even how to destroy all the Native Americans forever. At the same time it encouraged its citizens to settle the West, to become farmers, and to establish communities in the new territory, whether Indians lived there or not.

This chauvinistic policy was called "Manifest Destiny," and most Americans believed fervently that they had the God-given right — even the duty — to continue expanding the westward movement, to civilize the entire country, including the Indians.

On the other hand, the Indians believed they had a hereditary right to the land they had lived on for as long as they could remember. They did not understand the crazed land hunger of the man: living in the bad air of wooden houses and turning up the earth the wrong way with a plow. To become part of the white man' s civilization was not what the Indian wanted. He did not understand Christian religion with many gods in different churches. He preferred praying to one god, Wakan, the Great Spirit. Basically, the Indian wanted only to be left alone.

As Manifest Destiny became the controlling philosophy of the western movement, the Indian knew his way of life was doomed. Yet, he believed it was worth fighting for.

The Army Rattles Its Sabers

By the middle of the nineteenth century, many of the old fur trading posts and forts on the Missouri River were taken over by the military to emphasize the power and authority of the United States government and to provide protection for pioneers attracted to the beckoning west.

In the summer of 1855, a strong military contingent, called the "Sioux Expedition," under the command of General William Harney (for whom Harney Peak in the Black Hills is named) was sent to the plains to teach the Sioux a lesson. Harney and his calvary attacked a village of Brule Indians at Ash Hollow on the Platte River in Nebraska. Among the casualties were 86 Indians, including women and children. The U. S. Army lost four soldiers.

General Harney's unprovoked attack was meant as a retaliation for the so-called Grattan Massacre when the Brule Sioux had wiped out an entire detachment of thirty-two soldiers while the army was trying to arrest one warrior charged with shooting a stray cow of an immigrant train. Although called a massacre by the whites, these soldiers were certainly well-armed. This humiliating white man's defeat was regarded as the first outbreak of the Sioux Wars which lasted for about thirty years.

After the Ash Hollow victory, the cavalry rode to Fort Laramie, Wyoming Territory, where General Harney parleyed with some Sioux chiefs over their mutual problems in maintaining the peace. From there, Harney and his troopers went on a long horseback ride to Fort Pierre on the Missouri River. Here they spent an uncomfortable, cold winter at the dilapidated fur trading post which the government had purchased from Pierre Chouteau, Jr. The once-imposing fort was named for Chouteau, the prominent fur trader and steamboat pilot. The old fort had not been repaired and remodeled for army quarters, as Harney ordered. He was most displeased, as were the soldiers who often sang a barracks-room ballad:

"Oh we don't mind the marching nor the fighting do we fear,
But we'll never forgive old Harney for bringing us to Pierre."

In the spring of 1856 Harney (whom the Indians called "White Beard" or "Squaw Killer") moved his cavalry 185 miles downstream. Some of the best logs salvaged from the destruction of Fort Pierre were then floated down the river. These were used to build a strong base at the first military fort on the Upper Missouri, named Fort Randall, near present-day Pickstown, SD. Troopers considered accommodations at Fort Randall to be the "lap of luxury." More than twenty years later, Sitting Bull, after he returned from Canada and surrendered to American authorities, was confined at Fort Randall, but probably not luxuriously.

Sitting Bull and relatives. On his right is his mother, Her Holy Door.
Woman on left is his daughter, Has Many Horses.
The child is Tom Fly. The two women standing are unidentified

Photograph courtesy of the South Dakota State Historical Society

The wide-ranging military activities of General Harney in attacking the Brule Sioux at Ash Hollow, in parleying with Sioux chiefs at Fort Laramie, and in establishing a new military fort — at a strategic location — emphasized the new government policy of stronger involvement and more army participation in the affairs of the Dakota region and its inhabitants, both old and new.

Captain John Blair Smith Todd, Promoter

John Blair Smith Todd, prominent Yankton politican and first delegate to Congress from Dakota Territory

Photograph courtesy South Dakota State Historical Society

One of the officers who served under General Harney in the Sioux expedition and later became a trader or sutler at Fort Randall was Captain J.B.S. Todd who believed he saw a glittering future in land speculation and in developing portions of the Yankton Sioux lands. He resigned from the army in 1856 and became a trader in Dakota, looking for opportunities in the southeastern section of what eventually became Dakota Territory.

Captain Todd was a tall West Point graduate with a distinguished appearance accented by a silver-headed cane and white gloves. His suave manner, combined with an air of authority, was always impressive whether on the frontier or in Washington. Todd became a shrewd promoter and developer of Dakota by forming a trading company with Daniel Frost, a wealthy merchant from St. Louis. Soon the Frost-Todd Company became involved in trade with the Indians and in political maneuvering during pre-territorial days. For the rest of his life, Todd was one of the most powerful politicians in Dakota and influenced its history in many ways.

Before any land deals could be inaugurated, the whites had to extinguish the title to Indian land which the United States government was sworn to protect. The Frost-Todd Company was greatly in favor of helping the government negotiate and eventually ratify a treaty with the Yankton Sioux about selling their land.

Strike-the-Ree (Old Strike) was head chief of the Yankton Sioux. Todd knew he had an ally in Chief Strike-the-Ree, who was very tolerant of white men even though the chief knew they coveted the land of his ancient camp. Strike-the-Ree was the baby who was wrapped in the American flag and naturalized by Captain Meriwether Lewis on the day of his birth. According to the oft-told tale, the explorer had prophesied that the papoose he held in his arms would grow up to become a powerful leader and a true friend to the whites.

Chief Strike-the-Ree

Photograph courtesy South Dakota State Historical Society

Chief Strike-the-Ree spoke to his tribe of Yankton Sioux: "The white men are coming in like maggots. It is useless to resist them. They are many more than we are. We could not hope to stop them. Many of our brave warriors would be killed, our women and children left in sorrow, and still we would not stop them. We must accept it, get the best terms we can get and try to adopt their ways."

So spoke Chief Strike-the-Ree, according to author Robert Karolevitz. Not all of the Chief's people agreed with him and his attitude toward whites.

Charles Picotte—Half-Indian and Half-white

Another person Todd was counting on to help convince the Yanktons to sell their land was Charles Picotte, a half-breed who was the son of a French father from St. Louis and Mrs. Picotte-Galpin, an Indian woman noted for her aid to the whites.

Charles was also the grandson of a chief and a nephew of Chief Strike-the-Ree. When Charles was a young boy, he was sent to a boarding school at St. Joseph, Missouri.

Charles Picotte never forgot the sadness he felt when leaving his mother to go down the Missouri to a white school. As the boat steamed along, he could see her sitting on the bank sobbing dejectedly. The boy was just about to jump ashore when a man caught him. Then the men who were his chaperones tied him to three chairs; next they cut his long hair, which almost broke his heart.

Another vivid childhood experience he remembered was

Charles Picotte

Photograph courtesy South Dakota State Historical Society

being carried on his mother's back when drunken Indians were fighting over the liquor the traders had given them for furs. During the fight his mother had hidden him under buffalo robes in the back part of the lodge. The boy awoke to see a dead man, covered with blood, lying near him. Charles dashed out of the lodge as fast as he could, terrified. This experience of confronting a violent death made a lasting impression on the boy. Under the supervision of the Belgian missionary, Father DeSmet, Charles received a good liberal education at St. Joseph. When he was twenty-two years old the young man Picotte returned to his people, the Yanktons of the Upper Missouri.

According to author Renee Sansom-Flood and her intriguing collection of Yankton oral narratives, *Lessons From Chouteau Creek*, told and retold from one generation to the next, many of the current oral histories convey a dislike for Charles Picotte. He was regarded as the typical returned Indian student whom the whites admired for his "bicultural knowledge which he utilized in their favor." As he matured, Sansom-Flood reports from modern oral historians that he was often a braggart and show-off who lit cigars with a rolled-up twenty-dollar bill. He also delighted in tossing gold coins among a group of children to make them fight.

However, there were many Yanktons who liked and respected Charles Picotte. They believed that he sincerely agreed with his uncle, Chief Strike-the-Ree: that in order to prevent a terrible war which the Yanktons would certainly lose to the white man, the Indians should agree to a land cession.

The United States Government Requests Captain Todd Take Charge

During the preliminary negotiations about the Yanktons ceding their land, Captain Todd, who knew Picotte had considerable influence with the Yanktons, hired him as an interpreter. The two had become acquainted when Picotte had been an interpreter for the Harney Expedition.

Because Picotte was an expert in speaking and communicating

both in English and in Yankton Sioux, he was a highly effective interpreter and undoubtedly performed a service for the United States government that could not be duplicated. Whether the ratification of the treaty turned out to be beneficial for his tribe over the years is certainly debatable

Often, in communication between Indians and whites, as reported by nineteenth century contemporaries of both races, misunderstandings developed because the interpreters were not skillful enough linguists and often distorted, intentionally or unintentionally, the message they were assigned to convey. Not so with the fluent Picotte, who felt at ease with both races and their languages.

In December, 1857, Picotte, Todd, and Theophile Brugier, a white trader, accompanied a delegation of twelve Indians headed by Chief Strike-the-Ree to Washington, D.C. This group traveled by lumber wagons across Iowa in midwinter while undergoing many hardships and trials. Picotte recalled: "We had two wagons with four horses each. Sometimes we would break down, sometimes upset, and sometimes get stuck in the snow." At Iowa City, the hardy group boarded a train and arrived in Washington on January 1, 1858.

The Indian delegation remained in Washington until April 19, because most of the Indians, especially Chief Smutty Bear, simply did not want to sell their land. Picotte and Strike-the-Ree labored many long hours with powerful words to convince the others that the proposed treaty would be beneficial to the Indians. Years later Picotte summed up his reasoning; "We would have been the first Sioux to fight the whites instead of the Santees, if it had not been for that treaty."

The main reason for the delay in the decision was that Smutty Bear disliked the terms of the treaty and held off as long as he could, despite claiming to have received verbal and physical threats. At last Chief Smutty Bear did place his mark on the treaty even though he objected to many of the provisions until the day he died. Indian Commissioner Charles E. Mix signed for the United States.

Sansom-Flood concludes : "Smutty Bear never forgot nor forgave the suspected shady deals of Picotte and the easy accommodation of Struck-by-the-Ree." She speculates that if the oral history handed down was true, liquor was a deciding factor because Todd and Picotte were rumored to have kept the Indian delegates drunk most of the time, "insisting that its members would fall ill or die if they drank local water from Washington's elegant hotels."

During the long trip from Dakota to the nation's capital, the Yanktons couldn't help being impressed with the sheer number of white people "back in the States," — railroads, cities, tall buildings, and many other products of civilization they had observed on their journey. Perhaps Strike-the-Ree was right; there were too many whites, too much civilization, and too many guns to oppose them.

The final result of various types of persuasion was that a treaty was signed in April, 1858, known as the Yankton Cession by which the Yankton Sioux relinquished ownership rights to approximately fourteen million acres of land between the Missouri and the Big Sioux River on a line south of Fort Pierre to Lake Kampeska near present day Watertown, SD.

In payment by the United States government, the Indians were promised a reservation of 400,000 acres on the east bank of the Missouri River in what became known as the Greenwood Agency and $1,600,000 in annuities over a fifty-year period. Other promised benefits included establishment of Indian schools with a guaranteed education in "letters, agriculture, mechanic arts, and housewifery."

For Charles Picotte's "valuable services and liberality to the Yanktons" as stated in the treaty, he was granted 640 acres of land outside the reservation. He later selected his land grant on what became the original townsite of Yankton, SD, the new settlement for which Todd and Frost had so many grandiose schemes. Picotte also received $30,000 for his efforts in behalf of the treaty.

Many Yanktons were furious about the entire transaction, believing that Old Strike and Picotte were villainous traitors and insisted that they did not have the authority to make marks for the Indians who were not present at the signing. The feuds between the various factions continued for years.

The Last Day in Camp

On July 10, 1859, a year after the treaty had been signed, several thousand white "sooners" were impatiently waiting on the Nebraska side, expecting to cross the river and make their claims as soon as news came that the United States Senate had ratified the treaty. The Yanktons objected; they did not believe that the whites had any right to take over the ceded land until after the first anniversary of the signing. The misunderstanding between the two races was reaching a dangerous level even though they were separated by the deceptive Missouri River.

Smutty Bear was in a bad humor, still complaining about the treaty stipulations, and sent a rude message to Old Strike requesting him to move quickly to the reservation to receive his annuities because he (Smutty Bear) was now head chief of the Yanktons, one of the Seven Council Fires of the Dakotas. According to veteran historian George Kingsbury, Strike-the- Ree (which Kingsbury said was his correct name) responded "without any manifestation of ill humor" and said he was the Chief of the Yankton Sioux, and was so recognized by the "Great Father" at Washington.

A number of whites hiding in a nearby trading post watching the confrontation of the two powerful chiefs were certain there would be a battle. Instead, the two chiefs met face to face; Smutty Bear presented his grievances; Strike-the-Ree explained away Smutty Bear's objections and scolded him for pretending to be head chief. The council ended amicably with a traditional dog feast, a sign of brotherly affection. Two oxen also were roasted and devoured. Red Pipestone pipes were smoked and all was well. Strike-the-Ree's medicine was stronger than Smutty Bear's, and a revolt of the malcontents was averted before the steamboat carrying the first annuities arrived.

Ratification of the Treaty Brings Dramatic Changes

Waiting for the arrival of the steamboat were several thousand Yanktons — men, women, children, papooses — all living together in a huge semi-circle of about 600 tepees while preparing for the momentous move to another life. "Peace brooded all over," commented Kingsbury. The historian wrote in *The History of Dakota Territory:* "The time was approaching when the Indians were to surrender their domination and remove to their new homes on the reservation...and surrender their magnificent home in which their ancestors and themselves had been born and reared, and accept in its stead a paltry tenement, illy equipped and furnished, compared to the one surrendered."

Just as the camp heard the first far-away whistle of the steamboat, a band of several dozen painted warriors on horseback appeared, galloping about the immense half-moon of tepees in Strike-the-Ree's camp. They whooped and yelled while flourishing their knotted riding whips, probably to signify that the hour for leave-taking had come.

Then two aged squaws hobbled up a hill where the bodies of two honored braves lay on burial scaffolds. The women began chanting a dirge, and using bone tools, they dug a shallow grave. They then buried the remains in the earth of their ancestors. The women moved their hands symbolically over the grave; the ceremony was completed.

One wonders what Old Strike thought when he heard the whistle announcing the end of the old life. Would his people be content on the reservation? Was there enough room and freedom to hunt and fish? Would the Great Father keep the promises of the treaty?

The excited Yanktons crowded the shores, watching the approach of the fireboat-that-walks-on-water — its tall chimneys pouring out black smoke; the red, white and blue flag whipping in the breeze; the bell ringing; and the water churning as the white man's monster invaded their beloved camp.

The mass of Indians squeezed in as close as they could to the moored boat, the *Carrier*, to inspect the merchandise on deck. The new agent, Major Redfield, tantalized them by displaying annuity goods: food, gold and silver coins, colorful blankets and calico, bright beads. There was also an assortment of plows, wagons, mowers, a grist mill, but the Indians were not attracted to the strange farm implements they did not understand. Through an interpreter, Agent Redfield announced that he also had several thousand dollars to divide among them as the first installment on their annuities. The Yanktons were thrilled with the scene and the promises

When the *Carrier* steamed slowly up the river of no return, several thousand Yanktons struck camp. On foot and on horseback, they began pulling travois loaded with tepees, poles, buffalo robes, food, guns—all their belongings. The dusty caravan, composed of an entire tribe and led by Chief Strike-the-Ree, traveled in a long, orderly exodus of men, women, children, horses, and dogs. The mood changed from excited anticipation to resignation, even though the agent had promised them a feast of welcome upon their arrival at their new home sixty-five miles ahead.

As the Yanktons disappeared, the large "sooner" crowd who had been waiting eagerly on the Nebraska side of the river began paddling across in small boats and canoes to grab townsites and lay claim to the vacated land. The Frost-Todd men floated a forest of logs across the river to get ahead of the crowd by working all night marking off town lots and laying foundations for log houses.

On July 13, after three hot days of travel, the walkers and horsemen arrived at their destination by following the loops and curves of the Missouri. The river had long served as a wide and dangerous highway that brought together two divergent cultures which were destined to have numerous conflicts. As usual the Missouri River went its own sinuous way, oblivious to the history made on its wandering water and changeable shores.

When the *Carrier* reached the Greenwood agency site, Agent Redfield did not hand out the treaty goods immediately as the Indians had hoped he would. Instead, he stored the annuity merchandise under canvas until the work on temporary structures for storage was completed. Neither did he divide any money because he said it was not yet the right time. So the Yanktons, tired and disappointed, worked at setting up their tepee village. There is no record of whether Agent Redfield had a feast prepared to welcome the tribe to their new home, as he had promised.

Although there was no elaborate ceremony or proclamation on the day the Yanktons left Chief Strike-the-Ree's camp and the whites moved in to found the settlement of Yankton, July 10, 1859, may be considered the official opening of Dakota Territory.

New Way of Life at the Reservation

On the first Sunday that the Yanktons spent at Greenwood Reservation, Agent Alexander Redfield observed the occasion with an outdoor church service. He assembled the 2000 or so Yanktons to sit or stand in a large grassy area in the middle of the new tepee village. The agent read "The Holy Scriptures, the Episcopal Daily Prayer, and well-selected sermon," all presumably translated by an interpreter

Beef issue day at Standing Rock Reservation

From the picture collection of the State Historical Society of North Dakota

with a strong voice. This was the first formal Protestant Episcopal service in Dakota, but there is no record of how the audience responded.

Major Redfield (traditionally agents bore the title of major) stayed at his assignment for almost two years. Undoubtedly being the first agent for the Yanktons, who were themselves adjusting to reservation life, must have demanded a remarkable leader of unusual patience, understanding, efficiency, and integrity. Scanty information is available about Redfield's performance as an agent. During his first year he hired carpenters to erect a saw-mill, a stable, blacksmith shop, corn cribs, and a water lime cistern. Bridges and roads were also constructed on the beautiful and fertile land along the Missouri where many animals lived. Major Redfield did get into an angry confrontation with Charles Picotte who accused him of fraud. Then Redfield's son threw a goblet at the half-breed which cut his handsome face severely and knocked out a tooth.

According to the handed down oral narrations of the Yanktons, Redfield was not regarded as a good agent, but he had enough compassion before he left to give his cattle to the Yanktons to butcher. The departing agent knew his wards were suffering from hunger because of the late annuity boat.

Bishop Henry Whipple of Minnesota was an active crusader for the Indians in the 1860s. He often communicated with President Lincoln in person and by letters, writing to the president and protesting that agents were generally chosen for their positions without any regard for their fitness for the assignment. The Bishop pointed out that unless an agent was a man of the highest character, it was extremely difficult for him to maintain his honor because of the miserable salary ($1500 yearly) he received, scarcely enough to support himself and a family in an isolated region.

Indian agents received their appointments through the Spoils System when a new national administration came into power. Many accounts of agents and their management of Indian reservations describe how easy it was for an unscrupulous agent to amass a fortune. Often Congress did not make appropriations sufficient to fulfill the treaty obligations, which apparently were not of much concern to the legislative body. The Indian Bureau did have complex problems to solve, and it was constantly accused of corruption by other government bureaus, by the Indians themselves, and by the press.

However, James McLaughlin, the well-known agent at Standing Rock Reservation from 1881-1890, maintained that the Indian Bureau was often "shamefully maligned" and that it was taken for granted that because a man was an Indian agent, he was atuomatically a thief.

The Malfeasance of Dr. Walter Burleigh

The second Indian agent for Greenwood Reservation was an easterner from Pennsylvania, both a doctor and a lawyer, who was to become a powerful and controversial politician of Dakota Territory. In the spring of 1861 Dr. Walter Burleigh arrived with his attractive wife and children.

Dr. Walter Burleigh, doctor, lawyer, politician

Photograph courtesy South Dakota State Historical Society

Burleigh had campaigned in Pennsylvania for Lincoln's election and managed to arrange a visit to the White House after Lincoln took office. Although Burleigh boldly requested that he be appointed minister to the Court of St. James, Lincoln demurred and asked Burleigh how he would like an Indian agency in Dakota. When the President told Burleigh the salary was $2000, better than most agents received, Burleigh recalled later, "I told him right then and there that if I took my family out in that frontier country and only got $2000 a year, that I would have to starve or steal."

Lincoln was supposed to have responded dryly, "Dr. Burleigh, if I am any judge of human nature, you won't starve."

This revealing anecdote was reported by Zack Sutley, a long- time acquaintance of Burleigh who years later wrote a book about his frontier experiences, including his numerous adventures with Burleigh. Sutley recalled that Burleigh relished telling the Lincoln story himself and was proud rather than ashamed of the reputation he had acquired as an efficient swindler of Indians when he had been an agent.

Lincoln was surely right in his assessment of Burleigh; this aggressive man never starved.

Burleigh was a big vigorous man with a dual personality; when talking to President Lincoln (or anyone with influence), he could be charming, persuasive, and genteel. When talking with his charges, the Yanktons, or other people he regarded as unimportant, he was often crude and cruel. This energetic pioneer, who took giant steps both when striding around the reservation giving orders or later when intimidating rivals in the political arena, was consistently ruthless and would stop at nothing to gain an advantage, politically or financially.

The unfortunate Yanktons soon realized his duplicity and lack of concern for their problems. They reported that he had no ears because he never listed to them and, as their hatred increased, the Yanktons frequently pronounced his name "Bur-lie."

Burleigh mastered every trick to cheat both the Indians and the Indian Bureau of the annuities which were supposed to be used for the welfare of the reservation Indians. There were so many complaints about Burleigh's management of the reservation that an official was sent out from Washington to investigate the accusations.

The investigator was shocked by the audacity of the agent and awed by his imaginative frauds: Burleigh's daughter was on the payroll as a teacher to the Indian children although no school existed on the reservation, even though the Treaty of 1858 had promised one. Burleigh's thirteen-year-old son was paid eighty dollars a month as a clerk. Another son was paid a salary for hunting gophers. Burleigh's father-in-law, Andrew J. Falk (who eventually became Territorial Governor through Burleigh's influence), was listed on the records as a paid worker in addition to Burleigh's having licensed him and appointed him to be the Agency Trader with a monopoly.

In addition to the nepotism, there was evidence of Burleigh's staggering misappropriation of funds. Because of so many complaints and petitions against Burleigh as a corrupt Indian agent, President Lincoln suggested that charges be brought to a hearing as soon as possible. However, they never were for a number of reasons: political considerations by William Jayne, the first territorial governor; delays brought about by the Lincoln administration's concentration on the Civil War; the positive role played during the Sioux Uprising in Minnesota when Burleigh organized Indian scouts. Finally, the assassination of Abraham Lincoln ended any proposed legal action against the agent.

Burleigh cared not at all what people thought of him. According to South Dakota historian Doane Robinson, Burleigh often admitted jovially: "I gave the Indian half and took half myself." "Bur-lie" lived up to his Indian name because he often took more.

Historian Howard Lamar concludes, that with all of Burleigh's fraudulent schemes in various capacities, he stole $200,000 from Dakota Territory. After leaving his position as Greenwood agent in 1865, he moved to Yankton, the capital. There, he became embroiled in the lively and dangerous politics of the territory, and he intensified his rivalry with Captain J.B.S. Todd over trading posts and political posts.

While running for delegate to Congress, he distributed free chickens to voters. Burleigh defeated Captain Todd, the incumbent and served two terms. Eventually he moved to northern Dakota where he became involved in politics and in transportation projects. He was the contractor for the construction of fifty miles of the Northern Pacific railroad. Burleigh County where Bismarck is located was named for him.

There Were Some Good Agents

According to Elmer Cwach, who researched and wrote a thesis on the history of the Yankton Agency during the nineteenth century, there were a number of good agents at Greenwood.

Fortunately for the demoralized and disillusioned Yanktons, one of the best immediately followed Burleigh in 1865. He was P.H. Conger who reported to the Commissioner of Indian Affairs that he found the Indians "in a state of most abject destitution and poverty." When Conger left them, the Yanktons were growing crops, learning how to use agricultural tools, raising a large herd of cows paid for from their annuities, and demonstrating interest in learning new ways and methods. Mrs. Conger taught school in a special room with twenty to twenty-five children in daily attendance

At first Major Conger was disappointed when he found them unwilling to do any kind of work, "it being, in accordance with their customs and traditions, a great disgrace for a man to do any manual or menial labor." Conger was pleased when the Indians began to discover that labor brings rewards and honor instead of disgrace. Unfortunately, like other Dakota farmers, the Yanktons suffered from drought, grasshoppers, and poor crops.

Another capable agent was John Gassman, an Episcopal minister, who supervised the repair of agency buildings and taught the Indians to raise more cattle instead of slaughtering them too soon. Gassman also encouraged the Indians to build 250 houses from logs hewn at their saw-mill. He also helped them develop their talents for weaving willow baskets and spinning and weaving woolen goods.

Strike-the-Ree and History

Agent John Kinney, an outstanding agent during Strike-the-Ree's final years, wrote an interesting description of the Chief giving a speech, which he sent to the Commissioner of Indian Affairs in 1888:

Gifted with oratory which never failed to move his audience, and made forcible by his striking illustrations he spoke on great occasions in a loud tone of voice, always self possessed, never hesitating for a word, and in a manner so earnest, with words so incisive that he was able to carry the Indians with him.

Old Strike apparently had an ambivalent attitude about white man's education for Indians. Although he said he was against the school, nevertheless, he complained when the years went by and the government had not kept its treaty promise to build one.

Many Indians did not want their children to attend school and did not want English to be taught. When at last a school was built, Old Strike made a speech opposing it. But when Major Kinney loaned him a team and wagon, he drove around the reservation persuading parents to send their chldren to school. The agent's entreaties and Strike's powerful words increased attendance.

Through the years many of the other Sioux tribes continued objecting to the treaty. They said the Yanktons had no right to cede land that belonged to the entire Sioux Nation. It was common property that did not belong exclusively to the Yanktons, they claimed.

The whites knew that Chief Strike-the-Ree could always be relied upon to do his best to see that his people honored their promises to the Treaty of Cession. Included was a major stipulation that the "tribe would pledge themselves not to engage in hostilities with any other tribe or nation, unless in self- defense" and would "agree to deliver to the proper office of the United States all offenders against the Treaties, laws, or regulations of the United States." (These promises are the ones that Chief Smutty Bear disliked the most).

From the years following the Treaty throughout his life, Strike-the-Ree and his family were persecuted, insulted, and their lives were threatened. Old Strike, whom many grateful whites honored by calling "noblest Roman of them all," was shot at, his ponies slaughtered and disemboweled, his cabin destroyed. Despite the cruel treatment by the malcontents, Old Strike continued to maintain his patience and influence, apparently reassured by his own conscience and by the loyalty of many Yanktons that he had done the right thing in promoting the Treaty of Cession. Even an imperfect peace was preferable to war, especially if you feared being on the losing side.

Among historians, both Indians and white, there have been many disagreements about which form of the chief's name is correct and which is the proper spelling of his Indian name; it appears two different ways even on historical markers. Another main point of contention is whether he was born and baptized when Lewis and Clark visited the Yanktons in 1804 or whether he was already ten years old in that year. And when he died, was he eighty-four years old or ninety-four?

During the last two years of his life Old Strike was completely blind and very deaf. The date of his death is undisputed; it was July 29, 1888, one year before Statehood was achieved. Surely no one would object to the significance of the Biblical passage quoted by Reverend John Williamson at the funeral for the Chief: "Know ye not that there is a prince and a great man fallen this day in Israel?"

The Yankton Treaty of 1858, which meant so much to Chief Strike-the-Ree, was a historic landmark both for Indians and whites because it was the first cession made by any Sioux tribes in Dakota. Yankton, or Greenwood Reservation, was the first of the Sioux reservations to be established on the Missouri River. This momentous treaty

This monument is the tombstone of Padani Apapi—Struck by the Ree

Photograph courtesy South Dakota State Historical Society

opened the way to white settlement and increased the chances for Dakota to become a territory.

Captain Meriwether Lewis was right in 1804, fifty-four years before the treaty, when he had made such favorable predictions about the Yankton Sioux baby he had christened—whose formal Indian name was Pagani Apapi or Pa La Ne Pa Pe.

"Mandan Village and Bullboats" by Karl Bodmer from Travels in the Interior of North America by Maximilian

From the picture collection of the State Historical Society of North Dakota

"Assiniboin Breaking Camp at Fort Union" by Karl Bodmer from Travels in the Interior of North America by Maximilian

From the picture collection of the State Historical Society of North Dakota

PART FOUR

THE MAKING OF THE TWO DAKOTAS

Dakota Becomes a Territory

In the same years that the much-disputed 1858 Yankton Treaty of Cession was finally signed and ratified, and the Yankton tribe moved peaceably to Greenwood Reservation, some curious political activity of a different kind was taking place in southeastern Dakota. This choice location northeast of Yankton, although not where Dakota Territory was finally born, did experience some false labor pains.

Congress was considering creating a new state from Minnesota Territory. Involved in the geographical rearrangement of boundaries was a narrow strip between the Big Sioux River and the Missouri River, formerly part of Minnesota Territory. Land promoters were excited by the financial possibilities of this no man's land waiting for adoption by the Dakota Territory. The promoters dreamed of railroads and founding a settlement that would become the indisputable location of the territorial capital.

If these entrepreneurs could claim control of the area early, before the big rush, they were confident they would accumulate fortunes by the sale of this valuable land in a new territory.

Squatters Maneuver for Position and Power

As early as October, 1856, two Iowans representing the Western Town Company of Dubuque traveled to the falls of the Big Sioux River, an attractive location, about 75 miles north of the Yankton site. While they were admiring the scenery, a party of angry Sioux Indians told them to leave and "stay not beyond the rising of the morning sun." The whites obeyed.

Ignoring Indian threats, Iowan David Mills returned a few weeks later, built a cabin and staked his claim. The following spring, in 1857, he was joined by a group of Iowans; they claimed 320 acres for the Western Town Company and named the location Sioux Falls. Thus the Iowa group became the first squatters, those who settle on land without legal claim in hopes of gaining title.

A month later the Dakota Land Company of Minnesota, with Governor Medary of Minnesota Territory at its head, sent a group of squatters to the falls of the Big Sioux River. The Minnesota speculators were chagrined to find that the lovely falls and rich surrounding country were already staked out by the Iowans. However, there was plenty of land to go around, so they set up camp on an adjoining townsite which they christened Sioux Falls City.

The two competing squatter groups of adventurous young men managed to co-exist in peaceful rivalry and finally consolidated their forces. While exploring the countryside, they devised a fantastic hoax which involved appointing themselves as judges and clerks for imaginary elections, complete with stuffed ballot boxes. Wherever their horses stopped, they established election precincts and voted over and over again in their own names in addition to forging the signatures of friends and relatives.

The climax of this game of make-believe was that they elected a squatter legislator, a governor, and a territorial delegate to Congress. By this brazen approach, these "sooners" hoped to convince Congress that they had a good-sized population and could qualify to become a territory. Congress refused to recognize the ersatz territorial delegate, ignored all the ridiculous election frauds and scorned their appeals for recognition.

Undiscouraged by the Congressional reaction, the combined group strengthened their settlement at Sioux Falls, then established footholds at Flandreau and Medary. Chief Smutty Bear of the Yanktons, who was usually at odds with peace advocate Chief Strike-the-Ree, was determined to drive the new settlers away. He considered them trespassers because the Treaty of 1858 had not yet been ratified.

Missionary Dr. Thomas Williamson sent a warning to the group which eventually evacuated Medary and Flandreau. Later the Indians burned the buildings and crops of the Medary group. At this time of danger, Sioux Falls people decided to stay and were not attacked. Both Sioux Falls and Medary claim to be the first permanent white settlement in Dakota, founded in 1857.

Many of the frightened settlers rushed to Sioux Falls where all the pioneers worked to build "Fort Sod," a crude barricade made of logs and earth 100 feet square, with portholes through the three-foot-thick walls, and a United States flag made from old shirts flying over the fort. The flag was created by Mrs. John Goodwin, said to be the first white woman settler in Dakota. At this time no Indians threatened, but the constant fear of them in Minnesota and Dakota did nothing to encourage a rush of settlers.

On July 2, 1859, the first newspaper in Dakota, *The Dakota Democrat*, was published in Sioux Falls by Samuel J. Albright from St. Paul. He had also printed hand bills for the election of the "squatter legislation." Albright was among those nominated for the counterfeit governor and was an active force in the political activities of the squatters. Albright's motto for his newspaper was "We publish only when there is anything to print."

One of his news stories concerned the young politicians of the Minnesota and Iowa land companies who spent the winter of 1857-1858 "amid many privations and hardships." W. W. Brookings, the head of the Iowa group, froze his legs so badly that they both had to be amputated below the knees. With no surgical tools, Dr. J. L. Phillips, a recent medical school graduate, used a large butcher knife and a small tenon-saw for the crude surgery.

Albright concluded the account: "Marvelous as it may appear, the patient, lying upon a bed of buffalo robes in his floorless cabin, with none of the surroundings and comforts deemed indispensable to a sick room, not only survived the shock incident to the harsh surgery, but entirely regained his health."

The patient, W. W. Brookings, despite his handicap, became a prominent pioneer judge and legislator. Brookings County, South Dakota, and later the city of Brookings were named for him.

The two land companies from Minnesota and Iowa, which set up the offending political body, failed in their objectives to establish a recognized government before any additional settlers arrived. They had counted on support from the Democrats, but when Republican Abraham Lincoln was elected in 1860, their chances vanished. Nevertheless, the trespassers, despite their extralegal operations, understood the business opportunities that accompany a frontier government. When the genuine Dakota Territory came into being, they exerted lasting influence politically. Many of them were educated men — lawyers, journalists, a doctor, and other enterprising professions, including Judge W. W. Brookings, Judge Charles Flandrau, Samuel Albright, and Dr. J. L. Phillips.

Agitation for Dakota Territory Continues

Both land speculators and ambitious politicians increased agitation for Dakota Territory to become a fact, thus assuring the investors of many economic and political advantages if they could attract enough legitimate settlers to the unknown region. There were many obstacles to overcome. Even the word "Dakota" had an intimidating though romantic sound to it, perhaps associated with the formidable Sioux Indians and the gloomy "Great American Desert" theory circulated by Major Stephen Long after his explorations of the Great Plains.

If settlers were looking for the place "where the West begins," it was supposed to be in the middle of that wicked river, the Missouri, notorious for causing trouble wherever it zigzagged across Dakota. The location of Dakota in the farthest reaches of the frontier was a drawback to settlement and would probably have attracted more pioneers if it had been on the route of a well-rutted trail like the Oregon Trail through Nebraska Territory.

Still the few people who did choose Dakota liked it, praised its good points often with exaggeration, and encouraged others to join them, whether it was legal or not.

In November, 1859, on the site of Strike-the-Ree's old camp, Captain J. B. S. Todd, the promoter who had been in charge of negotiations for the Treaty of Cession, drafted the first memorial to Congress requesting territorial status.

Flourishing his silver-headed cane which dramatized his suave manner, Todd traveled by stage and train on the long trip to Washington and presented the Memorial to Congress himself. The legislators ignored his petition. In the tense pre-Civil War days, Congress had so many troubles with the slavery issue and trying to regain prosperity after the panic of 1857, it didn't pay much attention to what was going on "outside the states." Nor were they interested in which frontier group was currently requesting territorial status.

When Abraham Lincoln won the election in 1860, Captain Todd was quick to remind everyone that he was the first cousin of Mary Todd Lincoln. He was sure that the relationship would enable him to become governor. In January, 1861, Todd, persistent and determined, went back to Congress with a petition signed by 578 settlers in the southeastern corner of Dakota.

This time, to everyone's surprise, Congress quickly passed the Organic Act; and President Buchanan signed it on March 2, 1861, two days before his term of office ended. Previously, whenever an Organic Act had been approved to create a territory, Congress had to decide whether to include a "no slavery" clause in it. However, in an ironic contradiction and switch of tactics, both Republicans and Democrats ignored the slavery phrase and voted together.

In a hasty fashion, without debates or even a tally vote for Dakota, the Organic Acts for the territories of Dakota, Nevada, and Colorado were voted into existence. One explanation for the surprisingly quick and successful vote was that "the Republicans did more readily because they had full faith that slavery never could secure a foothold in any of the Territories named." Dakota became a Territory during a dramatic and tragic time in the nation's history. Two days after Dakota Territory became a fact, Abraham Lincoln was inaugurated President of the United States. The next month, April, the firing on Fort Sumter in South Carolina precipitated the Civil War, also known as the War Between the States and the Brothers War. The four years of the Civil War had a powerful effect on retarding the normal development within the territories.

Dakota Had a Varied Geographical Background

Dakota Territory, the largest territory in size, was now a vast unwieldy region, some 300,000 square miles or more, and included the area which later became the two Dakotas and also portions which later became parts of Idaho, Wyoming, and Montana.

For years Dakota had long been shifted and shuffled around like an orphan from one territory to another. At various times, it had been part of the following territories: Louisiana, Missouri, Michigan, Wisconsin, Iowa, Minnesota, and Nebraska. Now at last it was no longer "No Man's Land." It was officially Dakota Territory, named for the Dakota Sioux Indians who had lived there for many years after moving West from Minnesota. The word "Dakota" means allies of friends.

Celebration in the New Territory

The day the news of the birth of Dakota Territory came to Yankton was a memorable one for the 300 or so residents of the settlement which had already become the center of political life for Dakota. The long-awaited announcement was not flashed across the country in seconds; there were no telegraph lines north of St. Joseph, Missouri. Instead the news arrived in eleven days from Washington with the last lap by a lumbering ox team, but it revitalized the citizenry. Just how the northern settlers in Pembina in the Red River Valley bordering Canada learned of their new status is unknown.

"Shouts of joy that went up made the welkin ring and started a jack rabbit stampede for the distant bluffs," wrote George Kingsbury, the crusty author of *History of Dakota Territory*. He was a Yanktonian who observed history in the making, was one of the leading actors in the drama of Dakota, and later preserved its history for posterity.

Kingsbury reported: "There were handshakes that would abash a pump handle in energetic motion; songs were sung and jigs were danced and eloquent speeches.... There were no bonfires but an abundance of hot air and fervid words."

George Kingsbury, Yankton newspaper editor and historian

Photograph courtesy South Dakota State Historical Society

Moses Armstrong, the very first published historian in Dakota, author of *Early Empire Builders of the Great West*, was also an influential politician, surveyor, and author in Dakota. He added his usual witty comment: "There was an occasional drink of 'Bramble's Best' (Brambles was a general store with a tavern) which went down in legal and organized quantities."

Kingsbury summed up the significance and the celebration: "It was a never-to-be-forgotten occasion, and the enactment of the law was rightly regarded as an important step in Dakota's career.

Government in Dakota Territory Organized

The Northwest Ordinance of 1787 determined the rules and regulations on how the territorial governments should be organized. According to the Organic Act, Congress appointed the governor and selected the capital with the President's approval. The Territory was permitted to elect a delegate to Congress, to establish a Territorial assembly as the law-making body consisting of upper and lower houses, and the lower house could have as many as 26 elected representatives.

The 1787 Ordinance guaranteed that territorial status was temporary; therefore, territories could request statehood when qualified. The population of a territory had to reach 60,000 before citizens could apply for statehood. Only about 2,400 people lived in all of the sparse Dakota settlements so there was a long way to go to qualify for statehood.

Lincoln chose Dr. William Jayne, his family doctor and good friend, to be the first governor of Dakota Territory, even though Democratic Captain Todd, kin to the President's wife, had well-known aspirations to be governor. Dr. Jayne had some experience in local politics in Springfield, Illinois, but no background that prepared him to be the first governor of turbulent Dakota Territory.

Jayne was a tall, imposing man with piercing black eyes and a bushy beard. Only 35 years old when sworn in as governor of Dakota Territory in Washington in March, 1861, he was known for his quick temper and lack of political acumen.

Because Jayne may have suspected that Yankton would not be civilized enough to bring his wife and family, he deposited them for safekeeping at a one-story hotel in Sioux City, Iowa, and did not bring them to live in Dakota until a year later.

William Jayne, first governor of Dakota Territory 1861-1863

From the picture collection of the State Historical Society of North Dakota

Exercising his prerogative as governor, Jayne selected Yankton as the Territorial Capital instead of Sioux Falls or Vermillion which also vied for the honor. Captain Todd had lost out on his plan to become governor, but his town was chosen for capital. South Dakota State Historian Doane Robinson wrote in later years, without providing any documentation, that Yankton was chosen because of Mrs. Lincoln's intercession that her cousin's town be given preference for the honor.

At any rate, Governor Jayne and the other new territorial officials were not impressed with Yankton. The new capital city was a treeless village on a plateau beside the Missouri River. There were about 300 people who lived in rustic log cabins, shacks, or sod shanties. The streets were little better than muddy or dusty trails, but the town lots were marked off even though it was rumored they had questionable titles.

The Ash Hotel, the only hotel, also served meals. Mrs. Ash did the cooking and frequently served Missouri catfish, black strap molasses, and mush. The hotel was short of space, and the large rooms were divided into separate sleeping areas by animal hides hanging from the ceiling down to the hard-packed dirt floors.

Governor Jayne was fortunate that he had a small executive office in a cabin which doubled as his living quarters. Because of the shortage of rooms, he shared his cabin with Attorney General William Gleason, a dignified gentleman who often wore his top hat on the Yankton streets. Attorney General Gleason had to act as janitor and

North Yankton in 1874

From the picture collection of the State Historical Society of North Dakota

empty the slop buckets because the governor outranked him. These unsatisfactory living arrangements remained unchanged for six months.

Undoubtedly the Yankton populace was just as shocking to Governor Jayne and the new officials as were the accommodations and appearance of Yankton. The people were nothing like the upper-class citizens and well-dressed businessmen "back in the States." These youthful Yanktonians were unmarried, boisterous, and already accustomed to the rough life of the frontier. Many wore long hair, moustaches, and beards. They carried side arms and knives. Their bizarre costumes were a colorful mixture of Indian buckskins, pioneer hats and boots, and faded shirts from home. Motley was the word for the first body politic roaming the tiny new capital of the largest territory in the United States: lawyers, surveyors, trappers, traders, squaw men, Indians, half- breeds, speculators, land promoters, and army personnel from Fort Randall up the river.

Not many of these rowdy bachelors were interested in farming and agricultural opportunities. They were more intrigued by booming town lots, by trading with the Indians, by watching for the arrival of the next river boat and wagon train. The most popular diversion was holding drinking bouts followed by free-for-all brawls — anything to relieve the boredom of a small, isolated hamlet which was always in danger of running short of whiskey.

Then Governor Jayne and other dignitaries, as well as politicians arrrived. This turned out to be far more exciting than any other entertainment in Yankton. "Wide-open, red-hot, and mighty interesting" is the way journalist-politician Moses Armstrong described the political brouhaha which soon dominated the new capital.

From his executive office in the small log cabin, Governor Jayne's first official act was to order a complete census for Dakota Territory, to the top of the territory, and back down again, as far west as any white settlers could be found. He sent six census-takers who rode about 800 miles round trip on horseback to Pembina and other Red River Valley settlements. The census-takers arrived at a total popula-

Metis were half-breeds who were a mixture of mostly French-Canadian men who had married Chippewa wives. They traveled in huge caravans in Red River Carts loaded with supplies to hunt buffalo.

From the picture collection of the State Historical Society of North Dakota

tion figure of 2,376, including mixed bloods but not Indians. Pembina was believed to have a smaller count than anticipated because so many of their Metis, French-Indian half-breeds, were out hunting buffalo and could not be located.

After the census was completed, Governor Jayne divided the inhabited portions of the territory into legislative districts, created three judicial districts and appointed three judges, and ordered an election to be held to choose a delegate to Congress as well as the members of the first territorial assembly.

At last, Dakota Territory was on its way to becoming an active political entity. After Jayne had fulfilled his gubernatorial duties, he left Yankton for home in Springfield, Illinois, doubtlessly relieved. Most of the appointed officials left for more comfortable accommodations at home and in warmer climates. The citizens were displeased that their new officials didn't stay the winter and get better acquainted. This was a common complaint in all of the territories.

That September of 1861 the territorial populace, proud of its new status, was eager to cast its official and legal votes for the first time in Dakota. Historian Howard Lamar wrote: "Traditionally politically-minded, the American pioneer in Dakota was to make politics—the only organized general sport on the frontier—his main preoccupation throughout the territorial period."

Captain Todd ran for delegate to Congress as an Independent, hoping the Republican administration would forget he was really a Democrat and remember instead his relationship to President Lincoln. Todd trounced the candidates from Vermillion and Bon Homme. Todd was a respected leader who had engineered the 1858 Treaty of Cession and the successful Memorial to Congress. He relished being the delegate to Congress. Though he could not vote, he could debate, and the delegate always wielded considerable power and controlled political patronage in his territory.

Throughout the twenty-eight years of Dakota Territory, many prominent politicians vied for the office of delegate. Dakotans were not that concerned about voting within a particular party; they generally voted for the man. Personalities rather than earthy platforms—if they had one—continued to dominate the political scene until about the middle of the 1870s. This unfettered style of voting made politics more frustrating for the candidates, but it was also more of a game for the Dakota voters, and they loved all the chaos and uncertainty.

Moses Armstrong, that versatile pioneer, wrote in his *Early History of Dakota Territory* about the first election and how the candidates and speakers "attacked the bewildered voters with spread eagle speeches, torchlight parades, fife and drum and bottles labeled 'fire water.' " He described how the politicians traveled around the countryside in a cavalcade with belligerent musicians, lying lawyers, and cheering voters to do the drinking while listening to candidates brag. The political arena was a circus that never failed to entertain the electorate of Dakota Territory.

Moses Armstrong

From the picture collection of the State
Historical Society of North Dakota

The Pony Congress Meets for the First Time

By the spring of 1862, Yankton had grown enough that a local diarist proudly recorded that there were nineteen different buildings, including one hotel, two boarding houses, one saloon, one store, two legislative halls, a secretary's office, six occupied log cabins, and one unoccupied log cabin.

The first territorial legislature, called the Pony Congress because of its small size, met on St. Patrick's Day, March 17, 1862. The nine councilmen and thirteen representatives with an average age of thirty-two did not have much education, but they had a sense of responsibility about developing a sensible, workable government for their mammoth territory. The delegates arrived on foot, by horseback, and stagecoach. No one blamed Hugh Donaldson, the representative from Pembina, for being five days late because he had to travel on a dog sledge through wintery conditions over the vast 400-mile area that became the two Dakotas.

At first the two groups of the assembly met separately in available buildings. On the third day they met in a large cabin, made of cottonwood logs, that served as the Episcopal church. Governor Jayne had not yet returned from his winter vacation in Illinois so the secretary read his long, long message to the group. The Governor requested the legislature to provide adequate laws, both criminal and civil; to build educational, financial, electoral and military systems; to build roads, to prohibit Negro slavery but keep the Indians confined to the reservations; to conduct a geographical survey; to support the Union in the Civil War and work for the passage of the Homestead Act. Jayne's speech promised a great future for Dakota Territory and lifted everyone's spirits while they contemplated the glorious accomplishments to come.

Even if the speech was so long (7,054 words) that some fell asleep, the legislature was pleased with the contents they heard and ordered copies to be printed in four languages; English, Norwegian, German, and French, which represented the various nationalities that had been moving into the region in the past year and earlier.

The lawmakers realized they were laying the foundations for the future government of Dakota, and they decided that in many ways they resembled the Pilgrims at Plymouth Rock and the Founding Fathers. After contemplating these solemn thoughts, they got into a shouting contest over the permanent location of the capital.

Even though Governor Jayne had selected Yankton as capital, the legislature had the right to reject Jayne's choice, and a raucous debate took place as each booster of a particular town loudly extolled his choice. The arguments went on for days and assemblymen were getting hoarse from swearing and yelling. Speaker of the House George Pinney, ignoring his agreement with the Todd forces to support Yankton, suddenly sided with Pembina, Sioux Falls, and Vermillion to move the capital to Vermillion, which at that time was larger than Yankton.

Bedlam ruled the Assembly. The Todd group was betrayed and outraged. They tried to get a two-thirds vote to oust Speaker Pinney but failed. Then they connived to throw Pinney out the window, and while he was recovering from serious injuries, they thought there would be enough time to select a new speaker. Speaker Pinney heard

Dakota pioneers at a reunion in 1911 on the 50th anniversary of the founding of Dakota Territory. (back row from left) George Kingsbury; D.J. Holman; (front row from left) Horace T. Bailey; John H. Shobey, William Jayne, John R. Hanson

Photograph courtesy of the State Historical Society of South Dakota

of the plot and requested Governor Jayne, who had just recently returned to Yankton, to intervene.

Alarmed by the uproar, the Governor sent twenty men of the recently organized territorial militia to keep the peace. When the soldiers entered the house, the members adjourned in anger and demanded an explanation from the governor. In the confusion of accusations and denials, Jayne blamed Pinney for misrepresenting the facts to him and withdrew the militia. Pinney resigned as Speaker of the House and was replaced by twenty-two-year-old John Tiernan.

Frank Ziebach, editor of *The Dakotan*, described for his readers what he saw from his printing office. He noticed ex-speaker Pinney walk into a saloon; within a few seconds, out he came in a glass-shattering crash through the closed window and landed on the ground with the window sash around his neck. The editor saw "the sardonic countenance of Jim Somers behind him."

Somers, a giant in size, was the 23-year-old Sergeant-at-Arms in the assembly. He did not live a long life. Later, he marched into a saloon in Yankton and shot and wounded the sheriff. Shortly after that, he was killed in a gun fight at Chamberlain, D.T.

Another news item in the local press concerned Governor Jayne: "A real executive fist fight took place last night, at the Hotel D'Ash, between the Governor and the Honorable Jesse Wherry, late receiver of the land office. Hair-pulling, choking, striking, blood spitting and pugilistic exercises were the order, which were performed with grit and relish."

A few days later Captain Todd chanced to run into the ex-Speaker of the House, and personally attacked Pinney who "ran as few lawmakers can run," according to historian Doane Robinson.

Parliamentary procedure of the first Dakota Territorial Assembly was lenient and permissive. It allowed the use of a pistol shot to catch the Speaker's attention. The legislators frequently ordered drinks to be delivered to the assembly hall from a nearby saloon. Horseplay and fighting often mingled with serious matters of state.

Achievements of the Pony Congress

Despite the fights and disagreements, the Pony Congress in its 60-day session managed to conduct considerable business and passed a number of laws which had lasting influence into the statehood years. The legislators defined the boundaries of eighteen counties, organized the Dakota militia to protect settlers against attacks by Indians or Confederates, upheld the sanctity of the Sabbath, outlawed bawdy houses and gambling, provided for river ferries, and banned Indians from leaving the reservation without a pass. They also prohibited swine and stallions from running at large and awarded citizenship to half-breed interpreter Charles Picotte.

To soothe Vermillion for not becoming the capital, the Pony Congress promised it the territorial university, and the lawmakers awarded the penitentiary to Bon Homme.

Homestead Act Passed

The Pony Congress adjourned on May 16, 1862, and Congress passed the long-awaited Homestead Act on May 20, 1862. That act had immeasurable effect on the development of Dakota Territory and indeed, all of the vast frontier. The Act gave 160 acres of the public domain absolutely free (except for an $18 filing claim) to any citizen, man or woman, of the United States, or to any person of foreign birth living in the country who had declared his intention of becoming a citizen. After the head of a family lived on the land for five years and improved it, that person received the ownership title.

The Homestead Act sounded wonderful but at first it did not attract as many settlers as expected because so many men were fighting in the Civil War. After the War, the Act fulfilled its promise, luring thousands of pioneers to Dakota Territory and elsewhere, responding to the call of "Free Land."

The Sioux Uprising in Minnesota or War of the Outbreak

A tragic event which slowed up the settling of Dakota Territory was the Sioux Uprising in Minnesota. It also threatened Dakota, and was responsible for many settlers fleeing from the new territory without so much as a backward glance. Nor did the dreadful news of Indian attacks attract new settlers to follow the wagon trails to Dakota.

The causes of the Indian outbreak were the basic problems which continually caused mistrust and hatred between the two races. The Indians resented the broken treaties, and the unfair treatment by the government; the whites resented Indians for ignoring treaties, committing grisly killings, and rejecting advice on how to live like white men.

The Indian frontier in Minnesota was extremely combustible, mainly because of trouble over late annuities at the agencies even though there was food in the warehouses. At the Lower Agency in Minnesota, a large group of desperate Santees assembled, waiting for their annuities to buy food. According to the often-told account, Agent Andrew Myrich refused to give credit to the hungry Indians, saying "Let them eat grass."

The Sioux Uprising was triggered on August 17, 1862, by a trivial egg-stealing episode near Litchfield, Minnesota, when four young Santee braves shot three white men and two women.

Several angry bands of Indians, who felt they had been mistreated by agents, at last persuaded Chief Little Crow to lead the Santee Sioux in a bloody war to drive all white settlers from the beautiful Minnesota River Valley. The Indians were also aware that many white soldiers were away fighting each other in the Civil War. War parties began roaming the countryside killing and mutilating many innocent settlers, including women and children.The corpse of Agent Andrew Myrich was found shot in the back with grass stuffed into his mouth.

By the time the volunteer soldiers under Colonel Sibley had crushed the Indians' revolt, an estimated 500 to 800 whites had been killed at two battles at New Ulm, another at Fort Ridgley, and many other locations. No figures for Indian casualties were available. The day after Christmas in 1862, thirty-nine Santees were hanged at Mankato, MN, in a gruesome finale to the War of the Outbreak.

In Dakota Territory, eight days after the first killing in Minnesota, Indians shot Judge J. B. Amidon and his son near the village of Sioux Falls. Settlers who heard this frightening news vacated Sioux Falls, Bon Homme, and Vermillion and fled to Yankton where a hastily constructed stockade had been put together.

About 300 people crowded into the stockade or stayed nearby. Although uncomfortable and scared, they had enough food, water, and company. From a high bluff interpreter Charles Picotte watched constantly for smoke signals. Although it was rumored that some of the young Yankton braves were wild to leave the Greenwood Reservation and join the Santees, the forceful influence of Strike-the-Ree kept them under control.

The Sioux Uprising left lasting bitterness between the races. The downtrodden Indians had attacked all the whites they could find, and the settlers who survived, most of them peace-loving, responded with deep hatred for all Indians. The long-lasting repercussions were tragic.

Governor Jayne and Captain Todd Fight It Out

During the height of the Santee uprising, on September 1, 1862, Dakota voters went to the polls to choose a delegate for Congress. Governor Jayne, who had not completed the second year of his four-year governorship, decided he wanted to run for Congressional delegate against the powerful Captain Todd, the incumbent.

People wondered if the Governor thought both life and politics would be easier in Washington. Jayne, not noted for political finesse, did not try to unite the youthful Republican party, which he was supposed to lead. Instead, he encouraged them to become warring factions. Many citizens resented Jayne's hope to become involved in

Washington politics, and thus deserting the governorship. They interpreted his candidacy as an insult to Dakota Territory.

Republican Historian George Kingsbury, then the outspoken editor of the *Weekly Dakotan Union* described Jayne as a "political adventurer in Dakota, caring nothing and doing nothing for his people; a frightened non-resident who shunned the presence of all honest men and enjoyed the company of political villains."

However, historian Lynwood Oyos who wrote *Over a Century of Leadership, South Dakota Territoria and State Governors,* had a different opinion: "Jayne had successfully launched a governance system in Dakota despite mismanaged and fraudulent elections....With the Civil War raging in the East, he created a workable political system with little help from Washington."

The election was a mismanaged free-for-all with many irregularities and inconclusive results. There were no voters left in Sioux Falls; the village had been abandoned. At Fort Randall, a company of Iowa soldiers were supposed to be out picking wild plums; instead the soldiers located the nearest polling place to vote for Governor Jayne. In Charles Mix County where the Greenwood Reservation was located, half-breeds and non-residents were permitted to vote.

Up in the Red River Valley country, where the Democratic bloc was all for Todd, his supporters stuffed a hundred extra votes in the ballot box for their candidate just to be sure. Politicians on both sides tried to mislead the Norwegian settlers about their voting rights for the benefit of the individual parties. The bulging returns from the Red River Valley precincts arrived late because the messenger had to hide from hostile Indians.

At first, Jayne was declared the victor until the late Red River Valley votes were counted — all for Todd. Both candidates contested the election, accusing the other of chicanery. The fight carried over into the assembly where a wit suggested that both the campaigns and the election had focused on which of the candidates had the most influence with President Lincoln, his physician or his wife's cousin.

Election day, 1868, in Yankton

Photograph courtesy South Dakota State Historical Scoiety

At one point in the fiasco when it looked as though Jayne had won, he resigned the governorship and left for Washington to introduce himself as the new delegate from Dakota Territory. Secretary Hutchinson was appointed acting governor. Jayne served as the Congressional Delegate for over a year while the votes were counted and recounted and analyzed. The Congressional Committee on Elections, after studying the situation, decreed Todd to be the rightfully elected delegate: Todd—334 votes; Jayne—256. The late Red River Valley votes for Todd were accepted and 89 ballots were rejected as illegal.

Former Governor and Former Delegate William Jayne of Dakota Territory returned to his home in Springfield, to resume his medical practice. One wonders if he asked himself why he ever left Illinois.

President Lincoln appointed Newton Edmunds the second governor of Dakota Territory. Edmunds, the chief clerk in the Surveyor-General's office, already lived in Yankton and was familiar with

Dakota politics and with its ramifications. Observers believed he was the right man in the right place at the right time and was able to cope with the confusion caused by Jayne's departure for Washington after the mishandled election.

As for Captain Todd, he was again swinging his silver-headed cane down the Congressional aisles while bowing to his colleagues as though nothing had happened. Perhaps some Washington politicians wondered if the eccentricities of the crazy Missouri River they had heard so much about had anything to do with election behavior in Dakota Territory.

Fort Abercrombie on the Red River of the North

Fort Abercrombie, built in 1858, was the first federal fort in northern Dakota. The fort, consisting of barracks, officers' quarters, and a commissary, was constructed on the Red River near present-day Wahpeton, ND. The location provided a key point in the outer military defense line of Dakota and was the gateway to the Red River Valley and westward to the Missouri River. More a collection of buildings than a fortification, it also served as a rendezvous point for wagon trains going to Montana gold fields and provided protection for settlers in the surrounding fertile valley. For a few years, the fort was also a mail and supply station to the Twin Cities and to other posts and settlements in the new territory. At the time Abercrombie was built, it had no stockade and none was built until 1863.

A stockade had been desperately needed a year earlier. In September, 1862, the fort was attacked three times during the Sioux Uprising and withstood a siege by the Santee Sioux for several weeks. The commanding officer was Captain John Vander Horck of a Minnesota infantry regiment. While visiting a picket line, he was mistaken for an Indian, shot and painfully wounded. To take his place, a young lieutenant was put in command; under his leadership, the Indians continued to be repulsed. The Santees besieged the fort until September 23 when military reinforcements marched in from Minnesota and drove them away.

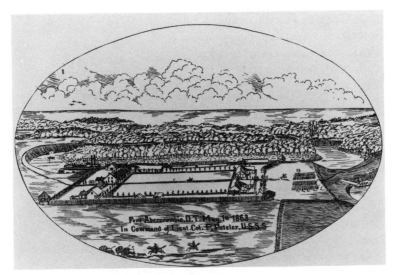

Fort Abercrombie, 1858

From the picture collection of the State Historical Society of North Dakota

According to a Sioux tale reported by both Indians and whites, during an exchange of heavy fire the Santees sent a message to the fort that they wished to see the one called Clear Sky who never missed, for they knew they were being shot down with a skill far above that of the ordinary soldier. The officer in charge responded that they had no one by that name, but the Indians knew better. The deadly marksmanship continued, and at last the Indians withdrew for they were convinced no man could survive a gun battle with Clear Sky.

The white man's name for their sharpshooter was Pierre Bottineau, a noted voyageur and frontiersman, who was probably the first white child born in northern Dakota, about 1812. Eventually, he guided James J. Hill, the Empire Builder, to map a route for the Great Northern railroad tracks in the wilderness.

Bottineau County where there were not a dozen settlers in 1882 is named for him, as is the city of Bottineau, ND. "Clear Sky, whose marksmanship and leadership were legendary, helped save Fort Abercrombie," the school children of North Dakota have learned from their history books.

Pierre Bottineau

From the picture collection of the State Historical Society of North Dakota

A year after the Sioux Uprising, when about forty settlers had been killed throughout Dakota Territory, the military expeditions of Generals Sully and Henry Sibley followed the Santee Indians who had escaped punishment in Minnesota by fleeing to northern Dakota. The military expeditions fought several battles with the Indians and subdued the red men for a few years, although the belief in Manifest Destiny continued to draw the whites westward and to make the Indians more belligerent.

Linda Slaughter, an Outstanding Pioneer at Fort Rice and Bismarck

Linda Slaughter, a pretty girl with long curly hair and a slim figure, was more depressed than excited as the steamboat ascended the Missouri River from Sioux City, Iowa, to northern Dakota. Battling the tricky currents of the Missouri, the steamer, *Katie P. Kountz*, made slow progress going upstream to its destination at Fort Rice, DT, about forty miles south of the settlement that became Bismarck.

Linda had been married two years to Dr. Frank Slaughter from Kentucky. His father had ninety slaves on his plantation but he fought for the Union against his brothers on the Confederate side in the Civil War. Now an army surgeon he was assigned to Fort Rice.

Linda Slaughter

From the picture collection of the State Historical Society of North Dakota

Linda was the daughter of a well-to-do family in Ohio, a graduate of Oberlin college, a professional writer, a fighter for women's suffrage, and had worked as a missionary to help free Negroes in the South. She had been planning to go to India as a missionary when she met Frank. Her varied background had not prepared her for the dangerous frontier of 1870 and the isolation surrounding the crude fort which became her home. She adjusted to her new environment and became an outstanding pioneer at Fort Rice, Bismarck, and throughout Dakota.

Dr. Slaughter later wrote in his unpublished autobiography: "I admired this young lady's writings, and no sooner saw her on horseback than I decided that a girl who could ride like that should not waste her life in India if I could help it."

Fort Rice, the first federal fort built on the Missouri in northern Dakota, was constructed in 1864 from cottonwood logs which were shipped up the Missouri on steamers. Built by the military forces of General Alfred Sully, the fort served as a supply base for the many divisions which accompanied the exploring and railroad surveying parties of the seventies. It was also the point of departure for Sully's

Indian campaigns, including the successful battle of Killdeer Mountain against the renegade Indians, the remnants of Chief Little Crow's marauding band from Minnesota.

On a steamboat trip up the Missouri, Linda was both fascinated and intimidated by the somber treeless plains stretching endlessly, by the knowledge that Fort Rice, surrounded by hostile Sioux Indians, was 836 miles from the nearest railroad at Sioux City, and many miles from Fort Sully and Yankton to the south, Fort Buford to the north, and Fort Abercrombie straight east.

She later wrote: "It is impossible to describe the dreadful feeling of solitude and impending danger that deepened as we steamed further and further up the river."

Linda, with her husband by her side, was relieved when the steamer, blowing its whistle and ringing the bell, maneuvered into Fort Rice landing. With her writer's eye for detail, she stored away the sights and sounds of the scene: The Stars and Stripes flying over the imposing fort high on a bluff overlooking the river, the rough stockade of planks surrounding the enclosure with cabins and buildings of raw cottonwood logs, the strange-looking Arikara Indians and their families staring at the strange-looking arrivals, the excited welcome of the military people who greeted them and cheered the boat's arrival.

After the Slaughters were settled with their baby and Negro servant in the officers' quarters, a sparse two-story cabin, with the chinks between the logs stuffed with mud, a chimney made of adobe brick and a handsome puncheon floor. They decided on a place to pile Linda's trunks stuffed with the finery of her wedding trousseau. Next, they took an inspection walk around the stockade. Immediately upon her arrival, an officer had warned Linda never to venture outside the fort alone. The Sioux, though often unseen, were always watching nearby.

In the barren prairie cemetery, Linda counted the graves—over 300 of them. Although some were women and children, most of the wooden slabs were men, marked "Killed by Indians." She was aware the red men had suffered grievous wrongs from the whites taking over their lands, despite the treaties. The Sioux were exceedingly fierce and vindictive toward the invaders for frightening away the huge herds of buffalo. During her many years in Dakota, Linda eventually learned that the tenets of the Indian religion were remarkably similar to Christianity and a belief in one God. Looking at the graves, Linda felt sorry for both races, dead or alive. At the same time, she feared the Sioux, and wisely so.

Dr. Frank Slaughter, the junior surgeon, made regular rounds just outside the fort to give medical attention to the sick squaws and children of the trusted Arikara (Ree) scouts who served the fort and lived in tepees outside the stockade. Often, Linda accompanied her husband, bringing food and small trifles in addition to sympathetic concern for the health of his patients. Many Arikara squaws spoke English, and they soon began calling Linda "the squaw that helps."

One day while Linda was riding horseback outside the fort with an officer by her side, a Sioux warrior with a gun sprang out of the bushes. Instantly, the officer grabbed her horse's bridle and urged both horses into a fast gallop. He fired his pistol at the Indian, who disappeared, and they escaped to safety through the quickly opened gates of the fort. The guards had observed the situation and knew what to do.

Isaiah, a Negro interpreter at Fort Rice, warned Linda that he had heard this particular Sioux vow during a scalp dance that he was determined to have the long curly hair of the white medicine man's squaw.

Some time later, an Arikara scout whom Linda knew came to see her, proudly holding up a fresh scalp with one ear attached which he said belonged to the Sioux who was after her scalp. Linda nearly fainted at the macabre sight. Her Indian friend was angry and insulted because she had not been overjoyed to see the bloody proof that he had killed her enemy. Although she didn't dance and sing, she mollified him somewhat with a bag of sugar.

Hardships at the fort were many. Decent food was often unavailable. At least the muddy Missouri River water was palatable after it had been filtered and the sediment had settled. In summer the mosquitoes were frightful. The wind blew all year. The hostile Sioux killed at least one mail carrier every season. In the winter there was an endless struggle with the cold and snow. Fire was always a threat.

Absolutely terrifying, day and night in the winter, were the starving wolves, who howled and danced on their hind legs trying to reach the top of the 10-foot-high stockade with their forepaws. The Ree scouts fired at the wolves continually.

Social life at the fort was highly prized. There were dances and parties, sewing bees, band concerts, special celebrations for every holiday, birthday and visitors— all these brightened the dull routine of every day life. Linda was never bored. In addition to devoting time to her growing family, there was a respectable library, and she kept occupied with her writing and painting.

On New Year's Day, 1872, Linda Slaughter's infant son Frank died. The baby could not be buried because the ground was frozen solid. Mrs. Crittenden, the wife of the commanding general, read the burial service; then the soldiers placed the tiny coffin in a powder magazine for safekeeping until spring.

The grief-stricken mother could not bear this arrangement so General Crittenden ordered fires built on top of cemetery ground where relays of enlisted men dug a deep, deep grave in the thawing earth and lowered the small coffin in a tin box. The soldiers, who frosted their eyelids and fingers, slowly poured buckets of water which froze immediately, forming thick layers of ice which no wolf could penetrate. Dr. Slaughter did not allow his wife to watch the burial ordeal. Later, Linda wrote: "As if in sympathy with the motive, the wind arose and tossed the snow about and heaped it above and around the little grave in heavy drifts that lay there undisturbed through the long cold winter."

In March the officers of the Seventeenth Infantry presented a beautiful silver cup to the bereaved parents. It had been intended for a Christmas present for baby Frank but didn't arrive in time. The Slaughters wrote a thank-you letter, concluding: "Until our own pul-

Main street of Bismarck in 1873

From the picture collection of the State Historical Society of North Dakota

ses are stilled in death's mystery, we shall treasure among our most cherished possessions, this little bright memento of our home at Fort Rice, with the officers of the 17th Infantry."

In the fall of 1872 Dr. Slaughter was transferred to Camp Hancock or Edwinton (later named Bismarck). While their quarters were being prepared, the Slaughters lived with their daughter in two big tents until a blizzard came. Then they moved temporarily into a fairly nice hotel.

At last their military quarters were ready. The Slaughters thought them truly handsome. Linda was especially pleased, because the four rooms were attractively papered with newspapers; the Slaughters read *The St. Paul Pioneer*, an army favorite and the outstanding journal of the northwest, over and over.

For Christmas Day, 1872, the Slaughters invited eleven boys and girls to Christmas dinner with a magnificent set of decorated elkhorns as centerpiece for the table. No Christmas tree could be found. Linda described the menu in her holiday feature for the *Bismarck Tribune*, northern Dakota's first newspaper: roast suckling pig, buffalo tongue sandwiches, bear steaks, and hot applejack made from canned apples and commissary brandy. For Christmas, 1874, the entree was beaver tail with baked beans. The branches of a buckbrush tied together made a fine Christmas tree.

Eventually, Dr. Slaughter resigned his army commission to enter private practice in the growing settlement of Bismarck. Without the servants Linda had been used to all her life, she had to learn how to do many things herself; take care of three children, cook in a drafty stove fired with green cottonwood, milk a cow, and raise pigs.

Even though Linda Slaughter worked as hard as any pioneer housewife and mother, she found time to accumulate many varied "Firsts." She organized the first Sunday school (non-denominational) held within northern Dakota. It met in a tent. She became the first school teacher and the first county superintendent of schools. When she lived in the

The Frank Slaughter family

From the picture collection of the State
Historical Society of North Dakota

hotel, she began a weekly reading circle that read aloud all the shorter plays of Shakespeare, each member taking a part. She organized the first Ladies' Historical Society and was elected its first president. Eventually the group incorporated as the North Dakota State History Society. Linda was honored to compose the first telegram sent from Edwinton.

She was the first postmistress, receiving a starting salary of twelve dollars per year. In this capacity, she listened to countless confidences of her patrons and wrote hundreds of letters for those who could not write. The Arikaras had given her an appropriate title when they called her "The Squaw That Helps."

Linda's own writing flourished. She wrote weekly letters to newspapers in New York City and other large cities, presenting Dakota in a favorable light. Her attitude toward the plains and prairies had changed since her arrival at Fort Rice. She had become a fervent promoter of Dakota and a believer in its future development, especially Bismarck.

From 1893 to 1894, she wrote a serial for the Bismarck Tribune. In 1972 this was published as a book entitled *Fortress to Farm* or *Twenty-three Years on the Frontier*, partly autobiographical and partly the early history of Bismarck. Hazel Eastman, Linda's granddaughter, edited the book and wrote an introduction and epilogue.

Clement C. Lounsberry

From the picture collection of the State Historical Society of North Dakota

In the years before Linda wrote these serials, an organization called the Burleigh County Pioneers was founded with Dr. Slaughter as president. According to Clement Lounsberry, historian and publisher of the *Bismarck Tribune*, "It was a bureau of immigration, a general intelligence office, and a board of trade." The association resolved to publish a pamphlet to advertise the country and elect a historian to write it. Naturally Linda Slaughter, the professional writer, was invited to become an honorary member as the only woman in the group.

Enthusiastically, she agreed to write the organization's pamphlet entitled "The New Northwest — A History of Bismarck and Vicinity." The *Tribune* printed two thousand copies which were circulated in large cities and read by many immigrants.

On the momentous day when the first Northern Pacific train was to arrive in Bismarck on June 5, 1873, Dr. Slaughter and Linda rode their horses out to meet the train. Almost the entire population of Bismarck was also on hand. The train stopped to take on water, and many passengers got off. Linda was introduced as "The Doctor's Wife" which is how she signed her newspaper letters. The immigrants, many from Minnesota, were familiar with her publicity letters and gave her so much applause and cordiality that all Linda could do was sit on her horse and let the tears roll down her cheeks. She had influenced them to come to Dakota!

Dr. Slaughter died of paralysis in 1896 when he was fifty-four years old. His obituary, reprinted in the *North Dakota Historian Quarterly*, said: "Dr. Slaughter was a typical southern gentlemen of the finest type, handsome, polished in manner, kindly in disposition and generous to a fault, a superb horseman and accomplished rifleman. While surgeon at Camp Hancock, he treated the citizens of the two gratuitously and his hand and purse were ever ready to relieve the wants of the poor and distressed."

During the fifteen years of Linda's widowhood, she was often in pain but continued to walk the streets of Bismarck with a cane, her long curls still intact. She lived to see many of her predictions about North Dakota realized and her visions of Bismarck as a cosmopolitan city on the prairies begin to come true.

When Linda Slaughter died in 1911 at age 68, her obituary in the *Fargo Forum* concluded its accolades with these words: "Her pen is the instrument that has carved her name in the annals of the early history of our state, where even ever-wearing time cannot erase it."

The *New Northwest* is today listed as one of the prized titles of Americana among book collectors and is included in the listing of

"Forty-two Fabulous American Books." An original copy—if one can be found—is highly valued because it was the first printed item published in North Dakota—a genuine western rarity—like the author herself.

Custer and the Seventh Cavalry Caught in Yankton Blizzard

General George Armstrong Custer considered it wonderful news when he learned that the Seventh Cavalry was being transferred to Dakota Territory. His wife Libbie did not share his enthusiasm. She wasn't sure where Dakota was, but she did know it was the hunting ground of the ferocious Sioux Indians whom she had heard even generals describe as "the finest light cavalry in the world."

Libbie asked, "What if the Sioux object to your coming and go on the warpath?"

The general laughed uproariously. "If the Sioux want a fight, we'll give them one !" He grabbed a saber hanging from an elk antler and slashed it back and forth lopping off imaginary heads. "The Seventh Cavalry can whip all the Indians in North American put together—you know that!"

Lieutenant Colonel Custer was the commanding officer of the Seventh Cavalry, but it was customary to address an officer by the highest temporary rank he had achieved. Custer had been breveted the youngest Union brigadier general (age 23) in the Civil War. Libbie always spoke and wrote of him as "the general."

It was a chaotic scene in the Custer household in Elizabethtown, Kentucky, when the orders came to move. For two years the Seventh Cavalry had been assigned to boring duty there, and the men were ready for some challenges. The general, as usual, celebrated every order to move with wild demonstrations of joy. He often smashed chairs and tossed his wife up in the air with sheer exuberance, Libbie later recalled in her first book, *Boots and Saddles, or Life in Dakota with General Custer.*

The Seventh Cavalry, in April, 1873, with some 900 officers and enlisted men, about 800 horses, 200 mules, Custer's numerous dogs, cages of mockingbirds and canaries, 40 laundresses, and the wives of a few officers, arrived by train from Cairo, Illinois, at Yankton: the end of the railroad, the 65-mile Dakota Southern spur which ran from Sioux City, Iowa.

The citizens of Yankton, the Dakota territorial capital, were thrilled and excited to welcome this first contingent of the Seventh Cavalry Regiment which set up camp about a mile from town. The Seventh planned to rest, then organize for the 500-mile horseback ride along the Missouri River northward to Fort Rice.

The Custer Expedition of 1874

Photograph courtesy of South Dakota State Historical Society

Many of the wives went uptown to stay at the hotels, but Libbie Custer with her Negro servants May and Ham, received the general's permission to rent a cozy little stoveless two-story cabin where they could store their luggage and other belongings. The spring-like weather changed in a twinkling, and before all these recent arrivals from the south knew what was happening, they were in the midst of a violent spring blizzard.

General Custer had been supervising setting up camp when the storm hit. He ordered the unprepared soldiers, whose tents kept blowing down as the visibility decreased, to move quickly on their own to find shelters for themselves and their horses in Yankton.

By the time Custer located his wife in the cabin with snow seeping through all the cracks, he was ready to collapse and had a high fever. Libbie sent for a doctor who managed to make his way through the swirling snow, prescribe medicine for Custer, and order him not to leave his bed. Custer was too sick to object.

The Custers and their servant couple had no heat and only scraps of food and candles. Outside, they heard the tramping of many feet and noisy bumpings against the house along with recognizable neighing, howling and braying of horses, dogs, and mules. The animals were lost in the storm, but there was no room inside to let them in.

A lighted candle in the window attracted bewildered soldiers who fell through the door when Mary and Ham pried it open. Libbie remembered the rolled-up carpets they had packed in Kentucky. There were enough so each poor frozen soldier could roll up in one to get warm. Afterwards, several of these men had to have feet and fingers amputated.

Libbie worried constantly about her adored general, who seldom became incapacitated. The 36 hours of imprisonment and isolation were a frightful nightmare to her. At last, the storm abated and rescuers in sleighs arrived with supplies and encouragement. Rescue teams also found the marooned laundresses and a newborn baby—all safe. Yankton people "were true to unvarying Western hospitality" as Libbie phrased it. They had helped avert a major calamity and they found shelters for many soldiers and their suffering animals.

Custer recovered his strength quickly and issued a proclamation thanking the Yankton populace for saving the lives of both humans and the essential cavalry horses.

After the weather returned to normal and the snow melted, the

*Seventh Cavalry officers and ladies
on the steps of the Custer house at Fort Abraham Lincoln.*

*Bloody Knife, Custer's favorite scout is on left. Libbie is next to him;
then seated is Maggie Calhoun, Custer's sister, her husband James
Calhoun is standing by right post. Tom Custer, Custer's brother is
seated at bottom left. General Custer is seated on far right.*

From the picture collection of the State Historical Society of North Dakota

townspeople, including Governor John Burbank, entertained the
Seventh Cavalry officers with a gala supper and fancy dress ball.

Custer was so impressed when he heard band leader Felix
Vinatieri of Yankton play "The Mocking Bird" on his violin that he
immediately persuaded this fine musician to accompany the Seventh
Cavalry to northern Dakota as their new bandmaster. (Vinatieri ac-

cepted, but after he survived the Battle of the Little Big Horn, he returned safely to Yankton).

To show their appreciation for the kindness of the Yankton citizens, the Seventh Cavalry presented a military review on an open plain. The audience arrived in every kind of vehicle, on horseback, and on foot to see the spectacular performance. The uniformed cavalry with Custer wearing a plumed helmet cavorted on beautiful, disciplined horses before a large crowd that looked as though all the settlers in Dakota Territory had gathered. "My heart swelled with pride to see our grand regiment all together once more and in such fine condition," wrote Libbie. She described the grand review: "The music of the band, the sun lighting up the polished steel of the arms and equipment and the hundreds of spirited horses going through the variety of evolutions which belong to a mounted regiment made a memorable scene for these isolated people. Besides they felt the sensation of possession when they knew that these troops had come to open the country and protect these more adventurous spirits who were already finding a place into which the railroad ran was too far east for them."

Felix Vinatieri of Yankton, Custer's bandmaster

Photo by S.J. Morrow, 1882, Yankton County Historical Society

The townspeople cheered and waved farewell when the ill-fated Seventh Cavalry rode away on their 500-mile journey to Fort Rice and eventually to their permanent post at Fort Lincoln. A steamboat accompanied the regiment along the river and brought the officers' wives, the laundresses and one baby, and many supplies. Libbie and Margaret Calhoun, Custer's sister, rode side-saddle beside their husbands all the way, visited the village of Two Bears, answered to reveille at 4 a.m., and slept in wagon ambulances like the troopers they were.

The Custer Expedition of 1874

In the summer of 1874, the United states government directed General Custer and his Seventh Cavalry to explore the Black Hills in southwestern Dakota to learn whether the rumors of gold were true and to find a suitable location for a military fort.

That the unknown region had long been declared off-limits to the white man mattered little to the political and military leaders of the nation. Ignored was the Laramie Treaty of 1868 guaranteeing the awesome shrine of sacred gods to the Sioux Indians.

The Custer Expedition of 1874 was organized at Fort Lincoln, on the Missouri River across from Bismarck, the home post of Custer's Seventh Calvary. The Expedition, reputed to be the best-equipped reconnaissance sent on a mission "outside the States" consisted of 1200 men including cavalry, infantry, and an engineering detachment. Also accompanying the group were five newspaper reporters, a galaxy of scientists, two professional miners, and photographer Illingworth whose excellent photographs are preserved. There were over 2000 animals including mules, horses, a beef herd, and Custer's dogs.

Custer had planned to take his wife with him on the Expedition and was outfitting an army ambulance wagon for her and her black servant Mary. However, at the last minute the news from the Ree scouts made him decide it was too dangerous. Later, Libbie Custer wrote: "Whatever peril might be awaiting me on the expedition, nothing could be equal to the suffering and suspense at home." She and the other wives were heartened when the Ree scouts brought mail back to Fort Lincoln four times during the two-month exploration with the saddle bags labeled "Black Hills Express."

The only woman with the Expedition was Sarah Campbell, a black cook whom the soldiers called "Aunt Sally." She cooked for the post trader, commonly called the sutler, who sold whiskey, food, and special provisions to the soldiers. Sarah Campbell thus was the first non-Indian woman, white or black, to see the Black Hills.

Aunt Sally was probably just as delighted as the men (many of whom recorded their reactions in diaries, letters, military reports, and newspaper accounts). They discovered that, as they traveled closer, the dry plains were transformed into the blue-green of pine-forested slopes. It was an oasis of sparkling water, painted canyons, and flower-bedecked valleys.

An unusual addition to a reconnaissance expedition was the 16-piece band, directed by Felix Vinatieri of Yankton. The musicians carried their instruments and rode on matched white horses. The Black Hills echoed with strains of "The Blue Danube," "The Mocking Bird," and operatic arias. The lender was inspired to compose "The Black Hills Polka" which the band often played when the mule teams got stuck or bridges had to be built or wagons lowered with ropes into gulches. The music drowned out the cursing.

Professor A. B. Donaldson, a botanist and St. Paul newspaper correspondent, wrote lyrical dispatches for his readers: "The music of the band was weird and fascinating.... It seemed to come from genii, concealed in the graves and caves of the mountain's side and fancy suggests the haunt of muses." He concluded the record of his first impressions with this paean: "The band played, and thus mingled with earthly and heavenly music, terrestrial beauty and celestial glory, the first day ends and the first night is ushered in to the strangers among the Black Hills."

Every night when Custer wasn't writing thirty or forty page letters to his darling Libbie, he wrote military reports which included paragraphs like this one: "It was a strange sight to glance back at the advancing columns of cavalry and behold the men with beautiful bouquets in their hands while the headgear of the horses was decorated

with wreaths of flowers, fit to crown a Queen of May.... I named this Floral Valley."

Surrounded by flowers and music, pine-covered mountains and cool rushing streams where the soldiers could bathe and wash clothes, no wonder the Seventh Cavalry felt they were on a picnic in a beautiful park instead of on a serious military mission.

At last the long train of wagons, men and animals reached French Creek just east of present day Custer, SD. Horatio Ross, an experienced miner, made the historic gold discovery in the creek. Then everyone, whether a mule-whacker or a scientist or a sutler's black

"A String of Pearls" describes the Custer Expedition wagon train in 1874.

Illingworth photo—South Dakota State Historical Society

cook, went wild, digging, scratching and panning gold with shovels, knives, picks—any available implement. William Curtis, the young star reporter for the *Chicago Inter-Ocean* and *New York World* reported the gold discovery at French Creek. He also interviewed Aunt Sally, describing her as "a huge mountain of dusky flesh and the most excited contestant in this chase after fortune."

Custer, in his military report, dated August 2, wrote ecstatically about the scenery, the spectacular views, the delicious wild berries, and the luxuriant grazing for the animals. Not until the end of the report did he casually mention that gold had been discovered in several locations.

Custer brought his wife a keg of delicious mountain water and specimens of gold and mica, fossils, and pressed flowers — even live rattlesnakes and horned toads.

GOLD!
THE LAND OF PROMISE
STIRRING NEWS FROM THE BLACK HILLS
THE GLITTERING TREASURE FOUND AT LAST
A BELT OF GOLD TERRITORY THIRTY MILES WIDE
THE PRECIOUS DUST FOUND IN THE GRASS
UNDER THE HORSES' FEET

With headlines like that throughout the nation, people began packing for the Black Hills — Treaty or no Treaty! The Black Hills Gold Rush had begun.

Aunt Sally Campbell vowed to return to the Black Hills and return she did, walking beside a wagon train from Bismarck. She lived at various settlements in Lawrence County: Crook City, Galena, Elk creek, and Roubaix. She cooked and midwifed for various familieis who expressed great love and respect for her. While puffing on her pipe, Aunt Sally entertained many friends who enjoyed listening to her tell and re-tell her adventures with the Custer Expedition. For many years she lived happily in the Black Hills among white people until her death at age 76 in 1888. She is buried in Vinegar Hill, a lovely little mountain cemetery in the tall pines west of Galena, a ghost town near Deadwood. Her large wooden grave marker says: "Aunt Sally — Sarah Campbell — Colored — She Ventured with the Vanguard of Civilization."

The significance of the Custer Expedition to the Black Hills was far-reaching. The team of scientists and miners had proved that rumors of gold in the Black Hills were true. From an almost completely unknown region, the Expedition had brought back valuable maps, photographs, and scientific information. From the white point of view, the Expedition was a great success.

Although Custer and his men had no encounters with hostile Indians, the Sioux had angrily watched from hidden observation points as the long military column wound through their sacred Paha Sapa. The presence of the Seventh Cavalry was a violation of the Laramie Treaty of 1868. The hated trail became known as "Thieves' Road" and provoked the growing fury of the Sioux Indians.

The gold fever was catching in 1874. War clouds loomed on the horizon. The Sacred Paha Sapa of the Sioux were doomed—and so was Custer.

Annie Tallent, the First White Woman in the Black Hills

The first white woman to enter the Black Hills was Annie Tallent, the only women with the 28-member Russell-Collins or Gordon Party. This group of "sooners" made secret preparations four months after the Custer Expedition, and in some areas followed his trail.

By entering the Hills, the Russell-Collins party ignored both the Laramie Treaty of 1868 and the United States government which ordered whites to stay out. Annie Tallent prayed they would not meet either the United States Army which escorted invaders out of the region or the belligerent Sioux who jealously guarded their Paha Sapa. She was constantly tormented by visions of the scalping knife.

Twenty-five years after the hazardous journey with her husband and her nine-year-old son, Mrs. Tallent wrote what has become the Bible of regional histories, *The Black Hills or Last Hunting Grounds of the Dacotahs*. The wagon train began the 78-day journey in late fall, and Annie walked beside the heavily loaded wagon through the plains and Badlands with gunny sacks tied around her worn shoes to protect her feet from the cold.

The group finally arrived at French Creek where the Custer Expedition had found gold. They built a stockade and spent a miserable Christmas, dreaming of home, surrounded by a forest of pine trees but no tasty food or gifts or decorations "nothing but picks, shovels, gold pans, and an ox chain for ornamentation." In January, 1875, the United States army tracked down these law-breakers and escorted them to Fort Laramie, Wyoming, with Annie riding a government mule. None of them had found significant gold under the ice in the creek or glittering in a snowdrift. When the Black Hills were later opened to settlement, Mrs. Tallent returned to live. Her husband deserted her, but she managed to support herself and her son. Active in church work, she be-

Annie Tallent

Photograph courtesy South Dakota State Historical Society

came an effective leader in several small communities; she was both teacher and postmistress at Rochford and eventually became superintendent of public instruction in Pennington County.

Mrs. Tallent has been accused of biased and malicious reporting about the Indians whose land she invaded, but she represented the attitudes of her era; that the Indians really had no rights—especially when it came to who owned the gold country.

Annie Tallent died in 1901, age 74, at Sturgis, SD, and was given what was reported to be a most impressive funeral by the Society of Black Hills Pioneers.

Gold Dust, Gold Nuggets, and Gold Diggings

The Indians knew about gold in the Black Hills long before the whites did. Traditionally, the Indians used the gold-flecked stones for sacred objects to protect the wearers and bring them good luck. The frontiersmen began to spread tales of Sioux Indians displaying nuggets from their buckskin pouches at Fort Laramie and at trading posts along the Missouri River where they traded nuggets for merchandise. True or not, the stories excited the whites.

According to many early accounts, Father DeSmet, in his travels among the Indians in the 1850s, often warned those living near the Black Hills and other gold regions never to show glittery rocks to whites because it would drive them crazy. For years there were constant rumors of the Black Hills being rich in gold.

In 1861, a month before Dakota Territory was created, a group of Yankton men organized the Black Hills Exploration and Mining Organization, but they never did more than organize. Although many eager dreamers on the frontier yearned to explore the Black Hills, they reluctantly obeyed the provisions of the Treaty of 1868. There was much talk of imploring Congress in one way or another to persuade the Sioux to cede their sacred Paha Sapa. Gold fever temperatures continued to shoot up higher as reports of gold West of the River increased.

After the Custer Expedition of 1874 had found gold in French Creek in the southern Hills, and the newspapers had proclaimed and exaggerated the news with banner GOLD headlines throughout the country, the Black Hills Gold Rush exploded even if it was an invasion of the Sioux Reservation.

The Russell-Collins or Gordon Party, originating in Sioux City, Iowa, secretly entered the Black Hills in the fall of 1874. The United States army escorted these intruders back to Fort Laramie where they were released with a scolding.

Throughout 1875, other gold-seekers broke into the Hills while evading the army who eventually gave up trying to stop the gold rush. The activity centered on the glory holes and streams which might be isolated gulches, and in the excavations in the villages springing up: from Custer City to Hill City; from Deadwood to Lead; and eventually to Hot Springs, Rapid City, and Spearfish. Converging on all the diggings with picks and shovels and sluice boxes were experienced miners and would-be miners. There were gamblers, prostitutes, doctors, lawyers, and promoters, journalists, suppliers, and at least one minister, Preacher Smith— all the floating population of the West.

Gold-seekers boarded the Union Pacific to ride as far as Sidney, Nebraska, or Cheyenne, Wyoming; they took the Northern Pacific to Bismarck; they rode steamboats up the Missouri River to Yankton, Fort Pierre, and Chamberlain. Then from all these exit points, they had to travel the last lap by stagecoach, wagon train, horseback or foot.

Yankton, Bismarck, and Fort Pierre all welcomed the business boom of the Gold Rush, and soon they became busy outfitting centers for all those rushing to the new El Dorado.

Supply boats steamed up the Big Muddy to Yankton and on to Fort Pierre. Here the crews of big Fred Evans and other freighters unloaded the supplies from the boats onto the waiting wagons.

Evans organized the first passenger and freight transportation train and later founded and built Hot Springs, South Dakota. He had the reputation for being able to swear an ox's horn off in two minutes.

Oxen and mules pulled these heavy loads for the fifteen-day trek over the prairies and through the gumbo to bring all kinds of merchandise to the fast-growing gold camps: mining equipment, a narrow-gauge train engine, portable saw mills, pianos, furniture, food, beer, and clothes. At Deadwood, which soon became the rip-roaring metropolis of the Black Hills, the wagons had to be lowered into the deep gulch by ropes, pulleys, and chains.

These gold-hunters from all over the country staked their claims, established businesses in tents, threw together crude shelters of canvas and evergreen branches, built log cabins and burrowed into dugouts under a cliff surrounded by the pine-forested mountains of the Black Hills. It was especially difficult to set up shacks, to maneuver wagons in narrow, twisting Deadwood gulch, where the mud mixed with garbage and animal excrement made a stinky mess. Many "pilgrims"— as the newcomers were often called— claimed they

Deadwood in 1876

Photograph courtesy South Dakota State Historical Society

could smell it two miles away. The year 1876, the magic year of the Gold Rush, was also the year of the nation's Centennial and the year of the Custer Battle. Miners found a considerable amount of loose gold in the Deadwood-Lead area which turned out to have the richest placer deposits in the world. The Manuel Brothers sold their hard-rock quartz claim to George Hearst of California for $70,000. Thus began the Homestake Mining Company of Lead, South Dakota, which became the largest gold producer in the western hemisphere from which millions of dollars in gold have been mined.

In June, 1876, Calamity Jane and Wild Bill Hickok, the two leading characters of the Gold Rush drama, galloped up Deadwood Gulch dressed in buckskins with long fringe and wearing white Stetsons and clean boots. Each sported two Colt revolvers, according to Richard Hughes, the first newspaper reporter in the Hills.

A yelling Calamity and a dignified Wild Bill were outriders for the Colorado Charley Utter wagon train, which had originated in Cheyenne, and was reportedly composed of about 190 people, including the first madams and prostitutes. The long ox-drawn train stopped the traffic in the crowded gold camp which had at least 70 saloons and

Wild Bill Hickok

Photograph courtesy South Dakota State Historical Society

an estimated population of over 5000. Gold dust was the medium of exchange.

Wild Bill and Calamity Jane were not lovers although they ended up side by side in Mount Moriah cemetery which overlooks Deadwood. Jack McCall, a conmon gun-slinger, shot Wild Bill Hickok, a U. S. Marshal from Kansas, in the back of the head in the Number 10 saloon. Wild Bill was playing poker at the time and held black aces and eights, known forever as the "Dead Man's Hand."

Calamity Jane was a prostitute with the proverbial heart of gold. She was a Good Samaritan who nursed the sick during small pox epidemics. She was also a scout, bullwhacker, and a colorful liar. Twenty-seven years after Wild Bill was murdered, Calamity died of alcoholism. Her dying request has long since passed into folklore: "Bury me beside Wild Bill, the only man I ever loved."

There were many pioneers who contributed much more to the development of the Black Hills

Calamity Jane

Photograph courtesy W.H. Over Museum, Vermillion, SD

than did those two whose lives have been transformed into legends and commercial properties.

Seth Bullock, the first sheriff and later a U. S. marshal, is credited with bringing law and order to brawling Deadwood without ever killing a man.... Bullock's long-time partner, Sol Star, was active in civilizing the gold camp and established the Board of Health. Star was elected mayor of Deadwood twelve times.... Dr. Flora Stanford of Deadwood was the first woman doctor in the Black Hills; a divorced woman, she began practicing medicine when she was fifty years old and drove her horse and buggy from Deadwood as far as Sundance, Wyoming, to care for her far-flung patients.... John Brennan, an Irish immigrant, had numerous firsts: in Palmer Gulch, he conducted the first miners' meeting ever held in the Hills; he was elected the first president of the city council in Rapid City; he was appointed the first postmaster of Rapid City and the first county superintendent of schools. He also

Seth Bullock, first sheriff of Deadwood

Photograph courtesy South Dakota State Historical Society

ran the first hotel in Rapid City in a one-room log cabin. John Brennan married Jennie Leedy who became a prominent civic leader, founding both the Baptist Church and the Young Women's Christian Association.

Dr. Valentine McGillycuddy was a physician, topographer, surveyor, a strong and honest Indian agent at Pine Ridge Reservation, member of the Joint Commission for the Constitutional Convention at

Bismarck, president of. the South Dakota School of Mines and mayor of Rapid City.

At the Pine Ridge reservation McGuillycuddy (called Father) and Red Cloud, chief of the Ogalallas, maintained a long feud, which both of these powerful men seemed to secretly enjoy. Red Cloud often delivered his famous pronouncement: "Father, and Great Spirit did not make us to work. He made us to hunt and fish....The white man can work if he wants to, but the Great Spirit did not make us to work. the white man owes us a living for

Dr. Valentine McGillycuddy

Photograph courtesy South Dakota State Historical Society

Red Cloud, Ogalalla Sioux Chief

Photograph courtesy South Dakota State Historical Society

the lands he has taken from us."

McGillycuddy was the first white man to climb Harney Peak, and his ashes are buried beside the stone steps leading to the look-out tower on top of this highest mountain east of the Rockies.

Gold was the magnet that attracted the white civilization to the Black Hills. Gold was the motivating force that developed the region and helped increase the population so that Dakota Territory could qualify for Statehood.

Libbie Custer Describes Life with General Custer in First Book

Eleven years after Custer's death at the Battle of the Little Big Horn, Mrs. Elizabeth Custer decided to write a book, the first of three, focusing on her last three years with her beloved husband whom she called Autie. His last assignment was Commanding Officer of the Seventh Cavalry whose home post was at Fort Abraham Lincoln across the Missouri River from Bismarck, D.T.

Entitled *Boots and Saddles or life in Dakota with General Custer*, it is "Dedicated to my Husband—The Echo of Whose Voice has been My Inspiration." Libbie, as she was usually called, describes the pleasures of going through life with her adored and adoring husband: the horseback rides together; the evenings spent beside him reading and writing in his study; the parties where Libbie, petite and pretty, stood by his side to welcome the officers and their wives, both friends and enemies, to be entertained with dances, charades, and card-playing; the hilarious practical jokes Custer and his family played on each other, herself included.

The Custers had no children but she loved being surrounded by the Custer relatives, especially the general's brother, Captain Tom Custer, who lived with them. How grateful she was for their excellent black servant Mary, who was also her friend. Libbie was thankful she did not have to cook or do housework. She enjoyed getting acquainted with Custer's favorite scouts, both Indian and white: Bloody Knife, Charley Reynolds, and Wild Bill Hickok.

After the Custer Expedition

Elizabeth "Libbie" Custer

Photograph courtesy South Dakota State Historical Society

of 1874, when Custer and his men had found gold in the Black Hills and had returned safely, she wrote: "From the clouds and gloom of those summer days, I walked again into the broad blaze of sunshine my husband's blithe spirit made."

Custer's cheerful presence and his devotion to Libbie made the disagreeable aspects of being an army wife more bearable at an isolated post in the wilderness. The Custer's first big house at the fort burned to the ground but a better one was built. Libbie was terrified of crossing the Missouri River, which she occasionally had to do in

General George Armstrong Custer

From the picture collection of the State
Historical Society of North Dakota

rickety boats. She tried not to look down into the swift current or admire the monstrous ice jams. The mosquitoes were unbearable (as all pioneers report). If the ladies in their long dresses wanted to sit on the porch in the summer, they had to douse themselves with ammonia and wrap their legs in newspapers for protection. In the winter the weather was frigid and blizzardy; in the summer, it was hot and dry; most of the time, it was windy.

The forty dogs Custer liked having around sometimes were a trial to Libbie; she liked them but not as much as her husband did. A pack of dogs always slept on the Custer bed or under it or around it; and puppies were often born and nursed on her counterpane.

But the very worst thing that could happen to Libbie was to be left behind at the fort while Custer was out in the field. All she could do was worry and pray for his safety.

On May 17, 1876, when the Seventh Cavalry left Fort Lincoln for its rendezvous with the other armies in Montana where the Yellowstone meets the Big Horn River, Libbie and her sister-in-law, Maggie Calhoun, rode beside their husbands for the first day's march. It was customary for the Seventh Cavalry to make a grand tour of the fort before leaving to bolster the spirits of the women, but often it had the opposite effect.

"My heart failed me," wrote Libbie when they approached Laundress Row to see the wives and children lining the road and crying, the mothers holding out the little ones for a last look at their fathers. Then the band, led by Felix Vinatieri, played "The Girl I Left Behind Me" and that was the worst hour while the tearful wives tried to smile and wave bravely.

Libbie, the General's wife, had to sit erect on her horse with her head held high, smiling and waving, to set an example for the other wives. She knew Autie would be ashamed of her if she wept and

Fort Abraham Lincoln in 1876

From the picture collection of the State Historical Society of North Dakota

displayed the emotions she felt so deeply. The well-equipped army with the colorful cavalry leading the way west looked formidable enough to intimidate any rebellious Sioux they might encounter.

Riding beside Autie, Libbie turned to look back at the two-mile-long column with the forked guidons of the Seventh Cavalry flying high. The sun broke through the early morning mist. A mirage formed, and in the haze appeared a nebulous vision of mounted solders, who seemed to be marching heavenward. The eerie vision soon vanished, leaving Libbie with the worst foreboding she had ever known.

Libbie reminded herself that Autie had made plans to have her join him later on when the last supply steamer would leave the fort and steam up the Missouri to the mouth of the Yellowstone. She would rather face any danger to be with him than to stay home waiting for news.

On June 25, 1876, many of the wives gathered at the Custer home to comfort each other and to share their feelings of despair. The women were filled with a sense of dread they could not dispel. There had been no news. Many wept openly in each others' arms; a few tried to sing hymns like "Nearer My God to Thee" – but it was no use. At that very hour, the Battle of the Little Big Horn was taking place "and the souls of those we thought upon were ascending to meet their Maker," wrote Libbie.

There had been numerous rumors that the Seventh Cavalry had met with disaster. Many of Custer's dogs had returned to the Fort. Some of the Ree Indians behaved strangely. A few deserted, as though they knew something the whites did not know. Undoubtedly, the "moccasin telegraph" had brought them news of the Indian victory by a combination of runners and smoke signals.

On July 5, the steamer, *The Far West* arrived at Fort Lincoln, bringing 51 wounded soldiers from the Reno-Benteen companies and the horse Comanche found on the Custer battlefield. Captain Grant Marsh, the noted Missouri River pilot, who could navigate on a "sea of dew," had made a fast trip, from the mouth of the Little Big Horn, to the Yellowstone,

The Steamer, Far West

From the picture collection of the State Historical Society of North Dakota

and then down the Missouri, navigating that dangerous river in fifty-four hours, a record never surpassed by a steamboat.

It was early in the morning when two officers and the post doctor arrived to break the news to Libbie, who had been lying sleepless on the bed, fully clothed. Although so greatly shocked by the tragic news that she nearly fainted, the General's wife was able to gather her strength and accompany the men to stand by while twenty-five other women were informed that they too were widows.

The *Bismarck Tribune* telegraphed the unbelievable scoop to a shocked and angry nation. Editor Clement Lounsberry wrote a 50,000 word story; the headlines were "General Custer and 261 Men Massacred."

Libbie lost her husband, George Armstrong, her brothers-in-law Tom Custer and Boston Custer, Custer's nephew Autie Reed, and Custer's brother-in-law James Calhoun.

Libbie lived fifty-seven years after Custer's death which occurred when he was thirty-seven and she was thirty-four. She devoted her life to honoring and bolstering his reputation while actively rejecting any criticism spoken or written about her hero. She died two days before her ninety-first birthday and outlived all his military critics. Libbie is buried beside her controversial general at West Point.

Truly, General Custer and his wife Elizabeth made American history — especially in Dakota, both north and south — where the long memories of them will never die.

Steamboating on the Red River of the North, Fargo and Grand Forks

Although there was traffic on the Red River as early as 1857, not until the Northern Pacific railroad bridged the Red River at Fargo in 1872 did steamboating boom and Fargo become the Southern terminus of river transportation. Only in the summer could steamboats be used. During winter in the 1870s mail and supplies were carried by pack horses and dog-sled.

Fargo, named for Fargo of the Wells-Fargo Express Company, was founded in the 1870s. It was immediately divided into two hostile communities:

Bismarck steamboat landing

From the picture collection of the State Historical Society of North Dakota

"Fargo on the Prairie" was an elaborate tent town, made as attractive and comfortable as possible for the railroad engineers and surveyors and their families. "Fargo in the Timber" was a miserable collection of dugouts, huts, and log houses along the wooded river banks. There lived the riff-raff who were often involved in drunken brawls and shoot-outs. These two sections of early Fargo had as little to do with each other as possible.

Fargo celebrated Christmas that first year, 1873, by ordering community Christmas trees, cut in the forests of Minnesota and transported in a box car to the village. That night the trees were stolen from outside the Headquarters Hotel. Fargoans suspected some Moorhead citizens across the river in Minnesota. Their effigies were hung from the new railroad bridge. The next night the trees mysteriously reappeared. So the Fargoans cut down the effigies, placing them in a box car draped in mourning. A solemn procession followed the engine pulling the box car to the bridge. Here the mourners removed the figures from the car and buried them ceremoniously in a snowdrift.

The holiday mood prevailed and the fun continued. Perhaps there was even some conviviality between the Prairie people and the Timber people. A tall pine was set up on Front Street, decorated with silver half dollars for every child under fourteen and lighted by an engine headlight. While everyone admired the sparkling tree, the children recited Christmas verses, then the outdoor audience sang Christmas carols in the snow. After St. Nicholas brought more gifts, the party moved inside to the Headquarters Hotel where the adults danced until morning. The children soon fell asleep on the hotel benches or snoozed in a corner. Fargo's first public Christmas celebration was a great success.

Fargo survived several disastrous fires, always rebuilding quickly. One hundred and sixty acres of buildings were destroyed in 1893. The Headquarters Hotel, which opened in 1873, burned several times and was rebuilt at least twice. Regularly, the Red River overflowed its banks. In 1897, the river flooded the whole valley. Many lives were lost and much property was destroyed. To save the railroad bridges of the Northern Pacific and the Great Northern from the raging flood, locomotives and threshing machines were cautiously run onto the bridges to hold them in place.

Fargo, from its very beginning, was a distribution and outfitting point for the thousands of homesteaders who came mostly by train to settle the country. In the heart of the rich black soil of the Red River Valley, Fargo continued growing to become the largest city in North Dakota.

Grand Forks, farther north at the confluence of the Red River and the Red Lake River, was first named Grandes Fourches by the French-Canadian explorers. In the early days it became an important station for river and oxcart traffic on the St. Paul-Fort Garry (Winnipeg) trail. In 1871, the mail came in once or twice a week by dog team. Grand Forks did not grow as rapidly as Fargo at first because it had no railroad.

Alexander Griggs is credited with being the founder of Grand Forks, and he also led the way in developing the community with his saw mill. Griggs built a squatter cabin at the mouth of the Red Lake River and also built the first frame house. In the first year of its existence, Grand Forks had a ferry, a stagecoach station, Griggs' saw mill, and a Hudson's Bay Company Store.

Griggs, an active and enterprising man, often piloted the steamer Selkirk which carried passengers from Canada to settle in the Forks. His clumsy flatboats and barges with heavy cargoes used to race up the Red River with pilots using many tricks to win.

When water flooded the basement of the *Grand Forks Herald*, the printers continued to put out the newspaper by hand. As in Fargo, the residents were often forced to live in second stories of houses and buildings and get supplies by crawling out their windows into boats. Farmers often constructed platforms with fences on barn roofs to corral their livestock. They brought hay to the animals by boat.

When the Great Northern Railroad reached Grand Forks

from Fargo in 1879, the steamboat traffic declined rapidly, as did the stagecoach traffic. The steamboat days soon became only a romantic and exciting memory on the Red River of the North.

Indian Legends about the Dakotas Abound

Indians of many tribes for centuries have been storytellers, and the elders of the village, who were often powerful speakers, would gather young people around a campfire. They would tell the story of a god, an ordinary person, a place, an animal, or food particularly, corn and wild rice. These legends were faithfully handed down from generation to generation in the marvelous oral tradition of the Indians.

Cause of the Breaking Up of the Ice in the Missouri River in Spring

All the Indian tribes in Dakota have legends, with some variations, about the mysterious monster named Miniwashitu that lives at the bottom of the Missouri River. In the spring the water monster moves upstream against the current to break up the ice of the river. Humans who have seen the uproar, if they do not lose their minds or die, describe the Miniwashitu as having a grotesque form covered all over with reddish buffalo hair, and one eye in the middle of its forehead with a single horn above the eye. Its backbone is jagged like a huge saw. Blazing like fire, the monster moves through the water with terrible roaring and booming sounds and causes the ice to build into jams, then to crash into the pile-up. And that is how the monster breaks up the ice of the Missouri River. As far back as anyone can remember, Miniwashitu has been feared by the people.

The Crazy Horse Vision on Bear Butte and Custer's Punishment

The Lakota Sioux have a legend about how the elder Crazy Horse had a vision when Wakan, the Great Spirit, appeared to him in the form of a bear on Bear Butte. Wakan endowed him with powers to overcome all obstacles and to vanquish all enemies. Because Crazy Horse was old, he asked permission to bestow these wonderful gifts on his young son, also named Crazy Horse, who then became strong enough to become a great Sioux leader. Many Sioux believe that the power bestowed on young Crazy Horse enabled him to destroy "Yellow Hair" Custer and all his troops in Custer's Last Stand. Custer was also punished because he had been audacious enough to camp with his expedition on "Thieves' Road" near Bear Butte, and he and his officers violated its sanctity by climbing the sacred butte and by photographing t.

Bear Butte, 1874

Illingworth photo
South Dakota State Historical Society

White Man Legends Are Scarce About the Dakotas

Ancient legends about the white man in the Dakotas do not exist because the white man hasn't occupied them long enough. Certainly, there were countless people in Dakota who have been described as legendary — explorers, pioneers, fur traders, politicians — but no accounts of their experiences have been in existence long enough to become a hoary legend, a truly ancient one passed down from the distant past, as Indian legends are.

The only category for which white Dakotans can qualify is in modern legends which had their start in the last two centuries. Most of these relatively recent legends are about gold in the Black Hills during territorial days.

Many intriguing ones involve "Fairy Gold," the name used to describe buried treasure in the Black Hills which was hidden either by its rightful owners or by highway robbers. Often those who were lugging the heavy gold had to get rid of it in a hurry to escape their pursuers.

That's where the legend begins. Where did they hide the gold? Underneath the floor of a deserted log cabin? At the bottom of a man-made lake (the only kind in the Black Hills) ? Underneath a pile of rocks? Among the roots of a tree? In a limestone cave? The possibilities are endless and fascinating.

The Holy Terror Mine in old Keystone about 1900

Photo courtesy Edwald Hayes

In 1878 the road agents who robbed the Deadwood treasure coach on the Cheyenne-Deadwood trail had to hide an estimated $100,000 to $250,000 of gold from the Homestake Mine when their wagon broke down. They had to stash the gold bricks in a hurry and run or ride for their lives. Two gold bars were reported to have been recovered but no details were available. If people find "Fairy Gold," do they report it? Perhaps finders want to be keepers and can keep a secret. Who knows?

A respectable legend that is aging well with a touch of the supernatural concerns the Holy Terror gold mine at Keystone in the Black Hills. It was discovered in 1894 by an Englishman named Rocky Mountain Franklin. He named it in honor of his wife, the Holy Terror. The weekly take was rumored to range anywhere from $10,000 to $70,000. The Holy Terror lived up to its name. Many miners have been killed in the mine by gas explosions, accidents, and floods. Several mythical creatures called trolls are reported living in the underwater mine. It is they who have caused all the trouble. To keep the rest of the high-grade ore intact, the trolls have locked up the "Fairy Gold" in impregnable treasure chests chained to the rich lodes on the rocky bottom.

A few hundred years from now, the story of the Holy Terror mine may become a genuine legend of gold in the Black Hills.

Paul Bunyan, Of Course

Although no one had read legends about Paul Bunyan before 1910, many good listeners had heard exciting tales of his exploits long before that. Paul Bunyan, American's favorite folk hero, was known as the personification of the glorified pioneer spirit. Perhaps he became a modern legend from an oral tradition resembling the Indians' storytelling style.

A mythical French-Canadian logger and lumberjack, Paul had no trouble at all taking a giant step over the Great Lakes, and another giant step over the Red River of the North. There he was in northern

Dakota where at that time there were altogether too many trees. Paul Bunyan, and his pet Babe, the Blue Ox, logged off northern Dakota in one month, and that is why North Dakota has so few trees today.

There are two legends about how Paul created the Black Hills. The saddest one is that Babe, the Blue Ox, died after eating four hundred pancakes and swallowing a red-hot, cast-iron stove. Paul cried so hard that tears flowed in rivulets from his eyes forming the Missouri, the Belle Fourche, and the Cheyenne Rivers. Paul decided it was too much work to dig a grave for Babe so he piled rocks and shoveled dirt on top of the smoking carcass until it was completely covered. In only a few centuries grass and pine trees began to sprout out of Babe's dirt-covered body—and that's one legend about how the Black Hills were created—by accident.

There's another legend called "The Mountain That Stood on its Head." It's a complicated story about the adventurers of the wonderful upside-down mountain where the loggers got dizzy from walking around upside down with their snuff boxes falling from their pockets.

Paul and his logging foreman Hels Helsen got into a violent fight over the predicament of the loggers. They struggled so furiously that the earth trembled and shook like an earthquake, smashing the mountain to pieces until it disappeared entirely. After the dust blew away into the Badlands (in both northern and southern Dakota), the two tired loggers were amazed to see that nothing was left except a cluster of black barren hills without one tree growing on them. Everyone was so grateful when the Black Hills improved a century at a time, and only pine trees that looked black from a distance began to grow into thick forests. Paul Bunyan hadn't meant to create the Black Hills—but there they were—by accident again.

Theodore Roosevelt in the Northern Badlands

"Up to 1880 the country through which the Little Missouri flows remained as wild and almost as unknown as it was when old explorers and fur traders crossed it in the early part of the century," wrote Theodore Roosevelt about the northern Dakota Badlands.

The first time Roosevelt, who became the 26th President, came to Dakota on the Northern Pacific was in 1883. He alighted at a little settlement later named Medora. To the cowboys, the New Yorker looked like an Eastern dude — a tenderfoot dressed in buckskins with a pearl-handled six-shooter on his hip. The cowboys regarded him as a joke from the East and soon nicknamed him "Four Eyes" because of his glasses.

Roosevelt came to Dakota to hunt buffalo and to improve his health, which had never been strong. On his first buffalo hunt with his new friend and guide Joe Ferris, the two hunters spent a miserable three days hunting stray buffaloes in cold and rain. Roosevelt missed shots and had continuous bad luck, but he refused to give up. He kept on doggedly and at last shot a big bull, to his intense delight. Already a good horseman, he had proved himself a hunter and a regular guy rather than a city dude.

Theodore Roosevelt

From the picture collection of the State Historical Society of North Dakota

Adding to his laurels was an incident in a saloon when a belligerent drunk cursed him and ordered him to buy drinks for the house. Roosevelt had to defend himself. An accomplished boxer, he hit the man in the jaw and knocked him out to the cheers of the frontier audience. That successful fight sent his reputation sky-high, and he gloried in it.

Before Roosevelt returned to New York, he bought the Chimney Butte ranch. Then he left his new ranch and cattle in charge of trusted frontier friends.

In New York, Roosevelt was elected to the State Assembly, thus beginning his political career. His health had improved during his stay in Dakota as a result of his active outdoor life.

Then double tragedy struck. After his daughter Alice was born on February 12, 1884, the next day Roosevelt's beloved wife Alice and his dear mother both died. To help him recover from his grief, he left his baby daughter in charge of his sister so that he could return to the ranch life that he loved.

On this second trip, he found the thriving new town of Medora, named for the wife of the Marquis de Mores, a French nobleman who had come to the Badlands in the same year as Roosevelt. Without knowing much about ranching or business, the Marquis impetuously decided to build a packing plant in the cattle country where the cattle would be butchered. The meat would be sent by refrigerated railroad cars to eastern markets, thus saving the ex-

*The Marquis de Mores
and his wife Medora*

From the picture collection of the State
Historical Society of North Dakota

pense of shipping live animals. The wealthy Marquis poured money into other ventures, too. He started a stagecoach line between Medora and Deadwood. None of his businesss enterprises was a success, but he left a lasting imprint on the small town. He built a church for his wife, Medora, a school, and an elegant chateau. The Marquis was in a gunfight involving several men, one of whom was killed. The Marquis was tried for murder but was acquitted.

There was great interest about how Theodore Roosevelt and the Marquis de Mores managed to live near such a small town. Several writers suggested that the two men were generally unfriendly and at one time were on the verge of fighting a duel. Other historical writers claim that in general the two were amicable, but there was always a strain because they were like "two very big toads in a very small puddle. "

Roosevelt spent his time learning how to run a ranch. He even enjoyed performing the various chores. One day on a roundup he instructed his men: "Hasten forward quickly there." The cowboys laughed so hard that their horses began to snicker.

Theodore Roosevelt's Elkhorn ranch

From the picture collection of the State Historical Society of North Dakota

By this time, Roosevelt had bought a second ranch, the Elk Horn, and had attained a reputation as a first-rate cowboy even if he was an Easterner. He made several hunting trips. On one he shot a huge grizzly in Wyoming. When he wasn't doing ranch chores, he was reading or writing books himself, including *The Winning of the West.*

He did not live continuously on the ranch but often returned to New York to pursue his successful political life. At age 28, he married Edith Carow, who bore him five more children.

In Dakota, Roosevelt became a deputy sheriff and was elected chairman of the Stockmen's Association. Ranching on the open range began to have serious drawbacks. Frightful blizzards with below-zero temperatures killed large numbers of cattle, including Roosevelt's. He eventually sold his ranch property and devoted himself to politics and to his wife.

When he left Dakota for good in about 1887, the *Sioux Falls Press* paid him a compliment: "Theodore Roosevelt is a Dakota cowboy." Many people had hoped he would run for Delegate to Congress from Dakota, but there were bigger things awaiting him. He left countless friends in the West River country.

After Roosevelt became President of the United States in 1901, the youngest man to serve in that office, he took the Northern Pacific on a western trip. It stopped in Medora and he later wrote: "The entire population of the Badlands down to the smallest baby had gathered to meet me." He made a statement North Dakotans have always cherished: "I have always said I never would have been President if it had not been for my experience in North Dakota.

Dakota Pioneers Had To Be Tough

The word pioneer is a heart-stirring word which suggests courage and ingenuity and problem-solving abilities. To survive in Dakota, pioneers had to be tough and resilient just to reach the Promised Land, let alone to stay there and battle nature. The hostility of the natural environment was demoralizing: the constant wind, the scorching heat, the frigid winters, the lack of plentiful water, and the treeless plains.

After the Homestead Act in 1862 and the end of the Civil War in 1865, the first pioneers began to come to Dakota by covered wagon, by available railroads, by boats and rafts up the Missouri and down the Red River of the North. Full of hope and determination on what wonders they could do with 160 acres of free land even if they had never farmed before.

Getting there was never easy. Many Yankees from "Back East" had to learn how to keep house in a cramped, uncomfortable covered wagon stuffed with tools, kitchen utensils, bedding, clothes, a few pieces of furniture, and trunks packed with previous mementoes of the homes they had left. There was no room to sleep except in tents or under the stars.

The husband drove the horses or the oxen, keeping his gun close by in case of an Indian attack or a chance to shoot wild game. The wife sat beside him on the seat, usually holding a baby. She had to keep close watch of the older children so they didn't fall off the end of the wagon or get lost when they straggled behind. Hanging underneath the wagon were buckets of water and often cream in a pail which would turn into butter from the bumpy movements. Every conceivable space on the sides of the wagon was utilized to hang a spade and a hoe and perhaps a treasured rocking chair.

The long, white covered-wagon train wound slowly across the Great Plains in what soon became rutted trails. The group camped out every night where there was wood and water if possible. There were no sanitary facilities. Women always answered the call of nature in pairs; one would stand in front of the other and spread out her long skirt to shield her friend, thus providing a little privacy. At night the campers built fires for cooking, for warmth and cheer, and often to dispel mosquitoes. The tired travelers would relax, exchange news of the day, and often would sing familiar hymns before settling down for the night:

Abide with me! Fast falls the eventide

The darkenss deepens—
Lord with me abide" was a favorite.

Pioneers, strengthened by hope and faith, in a wagon train searching for an unknown land, had to make many adjustments to cope with the dramas of life—love, birth and death—in an alien wilderness. Frequently, anguished families had to bury their loved ones wrapped in a quilt not far from a desolate trail, being sure to stamp down the earth and pile rocks on the grave to protect it from wolves and other marauders.

A wagon train winding its way in the ruts west of the Missouri River in southern Dakota.

Photograph courtesy South Dakota School of Mines Alumni Assoication

Many European immigrants had been attracted by the publicity circulated throughout Europe about the Garden of Eden atmosphere in a place called Dakota. Even though the immigrants could not speak English, they were eager to experience democracy and ownership of land. After an uncomfortable ocean voyage and a long wait at Ellis Island, they boarded trains in New York City with their names and destinations pinned to their clothes. They puzzled over the strange ways of America, including why a nickel was worth less than a smaller dime.

When they got off the train at a cluster of shacks beside a railroad track on the Dakotaprairies, they were often dumbfounded. Speaking in German or Danish or Norwegian or Swedish, they asked each other "Is this a town? Where are we? Where is the tall corn and the waving fields of wheat?"

Difficult as the adjustment was to being a pioneer in Dakota, how much harder it must have been for European immigrants than for white Americans from the eastern states.

Homestead of Benjamin and Helen Graham with son and daughter and probably the hired man. Young man with bicycle is author's father. Near Merricourt, North Dakota •
Second from left is Benj Graham followed by Helen Kellog Graham, Fred J. Graham and Ethel M. Graham.

Photograph courtesy of Helen Rezatto

O. W. Coursey, an American pioneer who became a prominent South Dakotan, wrote in *Pioneering in Dakota* how he, his father, and brother came together to Dakota from Illinois riding a long freight train, called an immigrant train. The three got off at the four-year-oldsettlement of Huron to file their claim. Mr. Coursey got busy and built a sod house with the help of neighbors. When his wife and six-month old baby and other children arrived, he was proud to show Mother her new home with its packed dirt floor and sod walls. At first she cried. Later she started singing and made them all feel better, her son recalled.

The Coursey family of eight lived in a one-room sod shanty, twelve by twenty feet. The kitchen, dining room, and living room were all one with a stove in the center. Two beds took up all the space in one end of the room, and the older children had to sleep on blankets on the floor.

Sod house built by pioneer Fred Nitsche in LaMoure county, ND

From the picture collection of the State Historical Society of North Dakota

The blizzard of 1888 is called the "School Children's Blizzard" because so many children throughout Dakota perished in it. It was understood that in a storm the children would stay at school. After a springlike day in January, a sudden blizzard struck with great ferocity over a vast area. In Carthage, South Dakota, the school board members collected all the rope they could find, tied it together, and fastened one end to the corner of a bank building. Hanging onto the rope for a guide, the men set off in the blinding snow to locate the schoolhouse. Although visibility was about zero, they found it. They tied the two youngest children to the teacher. With the men hanging onto the rope, they pulled the other children and the teacher by hand through the furious storm to the bank building. Here they all spent a cold night huddled together. The next morning the worried families were overjoyed to find everyone safe but hungry. (The original account was submitted to the South Dakota Historical Collections by the Prairie Tamers of Miner County.)

Homestead in blizzard

From the picture collection of the State Historical Society of North Dakota

Often a traveler caught in a surprise blizzard had to kill a horse or an ox and then crawl inside the butchered animal to keep from freezing. However, one man was found frozen solid inside the ox which had become his tomb, for the animal was encased in a sheet of ice and deep snow.

Everyone who lived in settlements along the Missouri River and the Red River of the North experienced frequent floods where the farmers lost everything but their land and their lives. Alice Bower Gossage described an awful scene in her diary when the town of Vermillion, SD, was destroyed in 1881. Watching from the top floor of her grandmother's house, the Bower family (The Bowers in the book, *The Family Band*) watched helplessly as their house floated down the Missouri. Alice wrote: "First the kitchen went, then the other part....the organ, my music....In short our home is gone and we are homeless." In March, massive ice chunks smashed all the steamboats wintering on the Missouri shores at Yankton. The steamboat industry never recovered. But the people in the southeastern corner of Dakota did not give up and go back east. New homesteaders continued to arrive. People began to rebuild their towns and farms. Because of the good soaking the farmland had received, the next crops were wonderful. The indomitable pioneer spirit of the Dakotans had never been stronger.

Prairie fires, raging for weeks, were the terror of Dakota during the summer and fall. The smoke would get so dense that the sun would be obliterated. Nina Farley Wishek of Ashley, North Dakota, a writer and teacher, described how, during a fire, the children were ordered to the middle of a plowed field and told to lie down with their faces to the ground. The Russian thistles would catch fire and bounce along, rolling balls of fire across the fire guards and igniting everything in their path. Many dreadful tales were told of parents trying to rescue their children who had caught fire; then all would be burned to death from the holocaust.

In 1889, the Statehood year, the April 4th headline on the *Mitchell Daily Republican* read "Mount Vernon No More!" The news story reported that despite brave men with brooms and shovels and wet gunny sacks fighting the enveloping flames of a prairie fir, the battle had been futile. Every business building and nearly all the residences were destroyed, together with about twenty freight cars and four large grain elevators. Only one human life was lost. Two churches and the schoolhouse escaped the fire. One hundred families were left homeless and destitute. A special train carrying provisions was sent out from Mitchell to the devastated town.

The almost demolished settlement recovered. The survivors rebuilt the town which rose phoenix-like from the ashes; and in 1989 Mount Vernon is celebrating the century and the centennial. No wonder the courageous spirit of Dakota has become legendary.

Almost a yearly torture to the pioneers were the grasshopper plagues. The 'hoppers stripped the cornfields, ate potatoes and cabbages right out of the ground, stripped the bark from young willows. The loathsome insects even halted trains with millions of them heaped on the tracks, making the rails so slippery that the tracks had to be sanded before trains could move. The stench of dead grasshoppers over the countryside was sickening.

In the horrible grasshopper year of 1874, Father Pierre Boucher led a pilgrimage of Catholics and Protestants seeking divine intervention in the grasshopper plague. They erected wooden crosses in three locations near the town of Jefferson, South Dakota. Their prayers were answered. The grasshoppers disappeared that miraculous day.

Rattlesnakes were a deadly menace West of the River even though the men scheduled rattlesnake hunts when hundreds would be killed intheir dens. Along with an invasion of mice, snakes found their way into the sod shanties and cabins. They coiled up in the beds, wound around the legs of chairs. The men taught the women and children how to be alert and how to defend themselves from lethal snake attacks with hoes, guns, rakes, rocks. One woman found a rattler wrapped around her sewing machine and managed to kill him before he could strike by an accurate stab through the head with a long knitting needle.

Many were the horrors of pioneer life.

Quilting party at the Pendroy home in McHenry County, northern Dakota Territory in 1883

From the picture collection of the State Historical Society of North Dakota

Perhaps to counteract the disasters and hardships the pioneers suffered, they enjoyed a good time: a long visit at a neighbor's house, an all-night dance with a midnight supper; quilting and barn-raising and spelling bees. They spoke a babel of languages and dialects, laughed at each others' funny accents, and the European immigrants struggled with American Indian tongue-twisters. They argued over plowing methods and politics and fought over the locations of county seats.

Although fiesty and opinionated, often divided by ethnic differences, these diverse settler learned to cooperate and combine skills to civilize their communities and the isolated farms and ranches. They established schools and churches, houses and outhouses, saloons and jails. They built roads and baseball fiedls and horsehshoe pits. Sometimes they took time out to admire the stunning blend of earth and Dakota sky.

Many early historians of the frontier, including Dakota, often wrote as as though only men had settled the West; and if a few women did straggle along, they were fearful and tormented like poor psychotic Beret in Rolvaag's saga *Giants in the Earth* whose husband Per Hansa was the personification of the pioneer spirit.

Women were seldom presented in either fiction or nonfiction as co-partners who contributed significantly to breaking in the Great Plains, a challenge formidable as trying to control a stampeding herd of wild horses. Nevertheless, the women managed to raise children without plumbing or conveniences and helped husbands do their work. Remarkably, most of them were able to create a comfortable home-place where a family could settle down comfortably–even in a sod shanty or a tarpaper shack.

Howard Lamar, a leading scholar of the American West and author of the book, *Dakota Territory*, has said: "The story of frontier is the story of ordinary people dealing with large problems. They overcame the problems and that is a symbol that ordinary man can cope with life....and that this country was developed by small, ordinary men, and not by supermen."

PART FIVE

THE MAKING OF THE TWO DAKOTAS

The Struggles and Strife Over Statehood

The citizens of Dakota Territory soon recovered from their ecstatic joy of being declared a bona fide territory instead of remaining an unorganized no-man's land. The government in Washington was beset with problems on how to win the Civil War and allotted less time than usual to helping new territories adjust to their roles. Despite the territorial confusion, tiny Yankton was proud to be the capital.

Dakota Territory, in its twenty-eight years of existence, was treated like a colony by a dictatorial Congress which exercised absolute control over all the hapless territories. Often the officials Congress sent out to govern the territories were corrupt, uninformed about the territory's problems, and concerned only with how to exploit these undeveloped regions "outside the states," control the patronage and become wealthy. It did not take long for ambitious local politicians who made up the power structure of Dakota Territory to resent this undemocratic approach which incorporated the worst features of the Spoils System.

Despite a few advantages like electing a Delegate to Congress and a Territorial Assembly, many citizens yearned toward Statehood which beckoned like a tantalizing star.

One of the most difficult hurdles for Dakota Territory to surmount to become a state was the 60,000 population requirement. In the first dozen years, settlers did not pour into the territory as had been hoped. In the early 1870s farming conditions were bad. Droughts, harsh winters, and grasshopper plagues contributed to starvation conditions among many farmers. Resultant unfavorable publicity—including Indian scares—did not attract eager settlers to Dakota. Many who had responded to the cry of "Free Land" had become homesteaders but had given up trying to make a living on 160 acres and returned to the East, disillusioned and broke.

Geographically, Dakota Territory was too big and unwieldy for either the United States government, the territorial government, or the scattering of citizens to cope with successfully, especially without adequate transportation and communication. How could the Pembina settlement in the northeast corner bordering Canada, and later the Black Hills in the West, and the southeast corner surrounding Yankton, learn to work together and discuss problems when only a few politicians managed to get a good look at each other?

Memorials to Congress Begin the Long Wait

Memorials to Congress urging the division of the huge territory were sent as early as 1858, the year of the Yankton Treaty of Cession. The half-breed Metis of Pembina and the Red River Valley forwarded a petition in French to Congress asking to become a separate territory named Chippewa, after the Indian tribe in the northeast. In 1871, members of the Territorial Assembly had unanimously signed a petition to Congress to divide Dakota into two territories. Memorials were sent to Congress in 1872, 1874, and 1879, emphasizing the need for territorial division. In 1877, the gold rush element in the Black Hills felt too isolated from Yankton to be taken seriously politically and requested that the Hills become the Territory of Lincoln. Another petition declared that Dakota should never be admitted to the Union as just one state.

Congress rejected all the various petitions without giving them much consideration. Those who had political ambitions thought statehood would provide more opportunities for jobs and patronage than territorial status.

Some politicians realized that statehood would be more expensive to live under because the national government paid the territorial bills. In statehood, the citizens would have to provide money through taxation to support a statement government. Yet statehood still had the most appeal to the emerging politicians as a means for improving the quality of life in the wilderness. How to stimulate Congressional interest and action on what the territorial leaders wanted seemed to be an unresolvable problem.

A Memorable Thanksgiving Dinner

Reverend Steward Sheldon of Yankton, an important missionary and religious leader, invited several prominent men to Thanksgiving dinner at his home in 1879. The potential of statehood was the main subject for discussion. Although none of the historical accounts mentions any women being present, let alone discussing anything of importance, the wives were presumably within the house. Undoubtedly, they were busy helping Mrs. Sheldon baste turkeys, serve the delicious meal, and wash dishes. Who knows; could they have been plotting women's suffrage in the kitchen?

Rev. Joseph Ward
author of SD state motto:
"Under God the people rule."

Photograph courtesy Yankton County
Historical Society

Males present at the Thanksgiving dinner included Dr. Joseph Ward (brother-in-law of the host), who has been described as the "prime mover in the whole statehood movement." He was a

Congregational minister and founder of Yankton College. Others included General W.H.H. Beadle, Superintendent of Public Instruction who "saved the school lands" and is known in both South and North Dakota history as "the patron saint of school children," Hugh Campbell, United States Attorney for Dakota Territory, a spirited crusader against what he called the tyranny of Congress and the author of the inflammatory "We Are a State" policy; Judge Alonzo Edgerton, chief justice of the Territorial Supreme Court, highly respected for his decisions except for the controversial ruling about the infamous Governor Nehemiah Ordway; Governor William Howard, an admirable governor, especially concerned for providing proper facilities for the care of the insane. (Governor Howard died before the statehood movement gained momentum.)

Governor Arthur C. Mellette of Dakota Territory Elected first governor of SD–1889

From the picture collection of the State Historical Society of North Dakota

This Thanksgiving dinner meeting was said to have been the true beginning of the statehood movement. These men attending became known as the "Yankton Oligarchy" and by their enemies as the "Yankton Ring." Their wives and many other enterprising women organized Statehood clubs to promote interest in the project. Although not present at the historic feast, a rising young politician, lawyer, and real estate agent named Arthur Mellette was also an important leader in the statehood movement. Mellette was the last governor of Dakota Territory and became the first governor of South Dakota. Described as sphinx-like because no one could guess what he was really thinking, he spent a generous amount of his own time and money in Washington promoting statehood.

Statehood Gains Momentum

The division and statehood movements gathered momentum in 1882 when a bipartisan division convention met in Fargo, elected delegates to visit Washington, and again petitioned for a northern Dakota territory. Sioux Falls, in the south, also held a convention to consider the best ways to promote statehood. Out in the Black Hills, the politicians had switched from advancing a territory of their own to considering statehood one way or another.

In 1882, a statehood convention (only ten counties were represented) was held at Canton, south of Sioux Falls, to push for statehood for southern Dakota. While the convention was in progress, a petition was being considered by Congress. At this time both houses were controlled by the Republicans so there was hope. Many southern Dakota party leaders objected to the Canton meeting because too many ministers who were for prohibition were attending. The opposition complained that the Women's Christian Temperance Union was holding a meeting at Canton the same week. Diplomatic Rev. Ward said the purpose of the convention was "to shape by friendly counseling together, the form of state government under which we are to live and our children are to be born."

To everyone's chagrin, Congress left this memorial for statehood as unfinished business on the docket, and certainly Dakotans agreed with that grim characterization. However, an important result of the Canton convention was the founding of the Dakota Citizens' League. It became a powerful group that worked for statehood and reform of the political system.

Unfortunately, the drive for statehood had not yet caught the popular imagination. Even though the politicians tried to keep the issue stirred up, they behaved as though attaining statehood was their special province. They did not try to include the farmers and uneducated people in their efforts. Many farmers were European immigrants who did not understand why a state was preferable to a territory, and language barriers made it difficult for them to comprehend the reasons for the political uproar.

Carroll Gardner Green who wrote a thesis entitled "The Struggles of South Dakota to Become a State" reported that "the reason for the loss of opportunity for statehood in 1882 was largely that of Yankton's County failing to satisfy her bond contracts." Also, Republican Senator Hale from Maine insisted "that the people of Dakota have not yet shown themselves capable of self-government unrestrained by federal supervision."

In the 1880s, the extension of the railroads into Dakota made possible the influx of many settlers into the Territory. The Northern Pacific railroad was awarded the largest federal land grant any railroad had ever received; its grant was actually one-fourth the area of what eventually became North Dakota, that is, nearly 18,000 miles. Thus, the Northern Pacific had land to sell the settlers they

The Northern Pacific railroad crossing the ferry on the Missouri River between Bismarck and Mandan.

From the picture collection of the State Historical Society of North Dakota

transported. This arrangement helped support the tremendous expenses in building a railroad that eventually spanned the distance from St. Paul to Seattle. (Before the Civil War, the Northern Pacific was built from Chicago to St. Paul).

In 1871, the rails of the Northern Pacific were completed to the Red River at Moorhead, Minnesota and bridged the Red River at Fargo the next year. The railroad went bankrupt in 1873, then borrowed money to extend the railroad to the Missouri River at Bismarck in 1873. Before a bridge spanned the Missouri, the trains crossed the river on barges in summer and on tracks laid on the ice in winter.

In 1879, the Northern Pacific began a highly successful advertising campaign in the United States and Europe. It advertised that the railroad would transport immigrants to the promised lush and well-watered land where crops grew to giant size in a Garden of Eden atmosphere with cheap land for sale. The railroad publicists had 831 local agents in the British Isles and a total of 124 agents in Norway, Sweden, Denmark, Holland, Switzerland, and Germany. Publicity was also carried in hundreds of newspapers in the United States to encourage more and more homesteaders or honyockers.

James J. Hill

From the picture collection of the State Historical Society of North Dakota

The Great Northern was the second most important railroad to come into northern Dakota. Built by James J. Hill, the Empire Builder, the tracks were laid in the Red River Valley from Fargo to Grand Forks, to Canada as well, and westward to Minot, with many branch lines.

Hill hired Pierre Bottineau, the noted frontiersman, as guide, and the two bearded, shaggy pioneers walked or snow-shoed from Winnipeg to St. Paul to decide where more rails should be laid.

Hill was a colorful character with great energy and vision. He did not try to build the Great Northern as rapidly as the Northern Pacific had done. Instead, Hill, with a pay-as-you-go philosophy, encouraged immigrants to settle the land only as fast as the railroad was built. Hill often bossed the job in person; he wanted to become acquainted with his workers. He would often step out of his private train, ask the men their names and where they were from, walk the grade, and give them a pat on the back to encourage good work. He insisted that the hundreds and often thousands of men lay the track at a minimum rate of a mile a day. In the heat and dust of summer, mosquitoes attacked in clouds causing horses to bolt and men and oxen to bellow in pain. The workers often collapsed from the heat and became ill from bad water. It was a harsh, difficult job to build railroads on the Great Plains and over the Rockies to the Pacific. The surveyors came first, often guarded by the United States Army to prevent Indian attacks. Later, when the actual work of laying the rails began, each gang of workers had specific jobs to do. They learned to work with precision and speed, and received good pay for a hard assignment under difficult conditions of weather, terrain, and human nature.

In southern Dakota no transcontinental railroad was built, but there was an exciting railroad-building race between the Chicago and Northwestern and the Chicago, Milwaukee and St. Paul (the Milwaukee Road). Which railroad would be the first to reach the Missouri River? The Chicago and Northwestern won because the crews of the Milwaukee Road got caught in an early snowstorm twenty miles from Chamberlain on the Big Muddy. Eventually the Milwaukee Road also reached the West Coast.

Plowing on the Dalrymple Bonanza farm in the Red River Valley 1875

From the picture collection of the State Historical Society of North Dakota

Bonanza Farms Boost the Economy

An amazing agricultural development stimulated by the Northern Pacific was Bonanza Farming in the fertile Red River Valley of northern Dakota. The Bonanzas began raising wheat on an enormous scale. These gigantic farms ranged in size from 3000 to 65,000 acres and produced No. One Hard, a strong durum wheat which grew wonderfully, brought favorable publicity to the area, and eventually encouraged small farmers to enlarge their wheat fields.

The Bonanza owners were eastern syndicates who hired managers to direct the mammoth operations. They required a small army of men and fleets of the most efficient farm machinery. No wonder the Red River Valley acquired the slogan "Bread Basket of the World."

*Harvesting on the Dalrymple Bonanza farm
in the Red River Valley 1875*

From the picture collection of the State Historical Society of North Dakota

Boom Years in Dakota

The years between 1878-1887 were known as the boom years in Dakota because of the great influx of settlers, the Homestead Act, Bonanza Farms, and the Black Hills Gold Rush.

During these good years, Dakota Territory had gone far beyond the population requirement of 60,000 to over 500,000. The politicians had more hope than ever of escaping from the territorial shackles. With increased optimism they worked harder than ever, convinced success was likely and soon. The Statehood Movement became more popular with the average person.

The courageous immigrants came to faraway and unknown Dakota not only from eastern states but from Norway, Sweden, Denmark, Finland, Germany, Russia, Ireland, Scotland, and England. These pioneers spoke a medley of different languages and brought a lasting treasure of ethnic diversity in customs and heritage. They made more of a delicious, spicy stew than a melting pot.

Governor Nehemiah Ordway, the most Controversial and Corrupt Governor

The venal Governor Ordway was a contrast to the beloved Governor William Howard who died in office and whom Ordway succeeded in May, 1880. President Rutherford Hayes appointed Ordway to complete Howard's term. Ordway, from New Hampshire, was a tall and

Governor Nehemiah Ordway

From the picture collection of the State Historical Society of North Dakota

distinguished-looking man with a pious air, but underneath his deceptive facade was a scheming mind full of duplicity and an obsession to become wealthy and powerful. Ordway was such a good character actor that he fooled the Yankton Oligarchy for a time before they realized he was as dangerous as a prairie rattlesnake and one who would strike without warning before he was molested.

Governor Ordway believed that Dakota should remain a territory but that Yankton should not remain as the capital: That's exactly what the Northern Pacific believed because it knew that a strong state government undoubtedly would try to exert more control than the territory over the railroad's activities. It was also what Alexander McKenzie believed even though he often insisted that he was not the tool of any man.

McKenzie was a sheriff in northern Dakota and a highly successful promoter for the Northern Pacific. A smooth, manipulative man, even though he could barely read or write, he was called Alexander the Great and eventually the Boss of North Dakota.

A man with a magnetic personality, he was both loved and hated but was regarded as the most interesting politician in Dakota. When he died, his funeral was held in the North Dakota capital building even though he had never held a state political office. The story goes that two grieving widows came forward to claim his million dollar estate, thus revealing that he was a bigamist.

Alexander McKenzie

From the picture collection of the State
Historical Society of North Dakota

Clement Lounsberry, author of *History of North Dakota*, wrote glowingly about McKenzie: "His name shall lead all others in writing of those responsible for the material development of North Dakota." Many historians apparently agree with Lounsberry on that point but disapprove of the methods McKenzie used to achieve his goals. Lounsberry, also the editor of the *Bismarck Tribune*, was the spokesman for the so-called Bismarck ring, which included the Northern Pacific, McKenzie, and finally Governor Ordway.

Even before Dakota Territorial days, Yankton had been the center of political and economic activity, mainly because it was located on the Missouri. As the population grew, Yankton's down- in-the-corner location became increasingly inconvenient for the far-flung sections of the Territory.

Travel was difficult between northern and southern settlements of the territory because of great distances. When the delegates to the Territorial Assembly traveled from Pembina to Yankton (400 miles), they had to come down the Red River as far as they could, then ride horseback or dog sled to reach the capital. After the coming of the railroads, Dakotans traveled by train on a roundabout loop via Minneapolis and St. Paul, and if coming to Yankton, got off the train at

Sioux City, Iowa, and rode the stage to Yankton (before the Dakota Southern reached Yankton).

There was considerable talk of moving the capital to a more central location; Huron was suggested as a possibility. Yankton knew it was doomed. Through McKenzie's and his railroad's influence, a bill was hurriedly passed in the Territorial Assembly empowering the governor to appoint a capital commission of nine members and let them decide where the new capital should be. When the public realized the significance of the bill, there was an uproar. All newspapers opposed the scheme, one editor claiming that not one newspaper upheld Governor Ordway "and the corrupt syndicate who have their paws on the throat of the capital."

The Capital on Wheels

The despised and undemocratic bill had this legal requirement; that the commission must meet, organize, and adjourn in the city of Yankton. Very quietly, McKenzie, whom Ordway had appointed as a member of the commission, arranged for the nine men, six from South Dakota and three from North Dakota, to rendezvous in Sioux City, Iowa, a railway center. During the dark of night, the men boarded a train furnished by the Milwaukee Road which arrived quietly in Yankton just as the sun was rising. With shades drawn, the group elected a president who then organized the meeting and presided over the election of a slate of officers. After completing the legal requirements about organization in Yankton, the group gave the engineer the go-ahead. The train blew its whistle and left Yankton without any of its citizens knowing the conspirators had been there.

B. J. Spalding, a Fargo lawyer and the youngest member of the group, wrote an account based on earlier notes of the whole affair. It was published in the *Bismarck Tribune* many years later.

Spalding wrote: "We visited each place and inspected the site offered, and at each we were entertained with at least one elaborate banquet," The candidates for the capital included Aberdeen, Redfield, Canton, Huron, Pierre, Steele, Fargo, Bismarck, Mitchell, Odes-

Burleigh J. Spalding

From the picture collection of the State
Historical Society of North Dakota

sa (Devil's Lake), Frankfort, and Ordway. The town selected was expected to donate $100,000 and 160 acres of land.

"At Pierre," Spalding wrote, "a unique celebration was staged. It included Sitting Bull and many members of his tribe. I recall that crowds of people gave a dollar each for the privilege of shaking hands with Sitting Bull."

Many of these settlements had little to offer except enthusiasm. Frankfort was the smallest settlement, and Odessa had only one business building. At Ordway, which was assumed to be the governor's choice because he was known to own considerable land there, his bustling little namesake town was sure it would be chosen. Speculators were making plans to build a large hotel.

Spalding's account continued: "There was no serious thought of the Bismarck bid being considered until we, in due course, visited that city."

The train and its controversial group also carried wives of the commission members, several Congressmen, and land speculators. They were greeted in Bismarck by the Eleventh Infantry band from Fort Keogh (Miles City, Montana) and many Indians from the Standing Rock reservation. Two banquets were set up with strawberries for dessert and with champagne flowing freely, Spalding recalled.

When the Fargo politicians learned about the expensive fete staged by Bismarck to influence the commission, they were furious and sent a letter of indignant protest signed by every important man in Fargo.

While traveling from Bismarck to St. Paul, the special train stopped for a time at Fargo. Spalding was in a hotel lobby inspecting a map when McKenzie saw him. This is how Spalding described the encounter he had with McKenzie later that day: "That evening, after I had retired to my berth, McKenzie came to see me and with much fervor and less tact upbraided me for examining the map and apparently assumed that I had promised to vote for some other location than Bismarck. Naturally and foolishly, I got mad and told McKenzie that I could cast my own vote. I believe he never forgot this incident."

In his long account, Spalding reports nothing more about McKenzie trying to apply pressure. However, in the last paragraph, Spalding writes: "To the resourcefulness of Alexander McKenzie, aided and supported by General Alexander Hughes, president of the commission, the people of Bismarck and of the state are indebted for what has proved to be an acceptable location....While his methods were not always above criticism there is little doubt of Mr. McKenzie's loyalty to what later became our state; and of his desire to serve it to the utmost of his ability."

Many people would argue that McKenzie's motives were never altruistic. He was a well-paid employee of the Northern Pacific to whom he was loyal, not northern Dakota. Did Spalding reveal the whole story or not?

Carroll Gardner Green, in her thesis about statehood struggles, reported that mystery surrounds the fact of Bismarck's becoming the capital, that non-partisan accounts of the matter were impossible to find, and "that it was done through graft."

Herbert Schell, eminent historian wrote in History of South Dakota: "The parliamentary maneuvers behind the capital removal in 1883 are not altogether clear; moreover, many writers have exaggerated the melodramatic aspects in the effort to cast in villainous roles both Governor Ordway and Alexander Mckenzie...Whether he masterminded the proceedings or not, the Governor certainly participated in a combination against Yankton. He may have desired to place the capital in a location of his own choosing for private gain."

On June 2, 1873, the commission met in Fargo to make a decision.

On the thirteenth ballot, Bismarck won with five votes. Redfield received two votes with Huron and Mitchell receiving one each. Spalding voted for Redfield.

Yankton was furious—especially the Yankton Oligarchy—not so much with the loss of the capital which they knew was coming but with McKenzie's sneaky manner in handling the commission's fulfillment of the legal requirement to meet in Yankton, without any Yantonian knowing the group had been there. That Bismarck won was a galling blow to the losing towns. There were many conflicting accounts of the "Capital on Wheels" deception. Yankton, in fact, most of southern Dakota and later South Dakota never forgave Bismarck and northern Dakota for "stealing the capital," even after statehood had been achieved.

The fighting and name-calling over the movement of the capital and of Bismarck's selection was the most violent political battle that ever took place in Dakota Territory. The transfer had both immediate and long-term effects. At first, many stubborn state officials would not join the hated Governor Ordway in Bismarck, four hundred miles away. James Teller, Territorial Secretary, protesting loudly, complained the longest before finally moving to Bismarck. However, he refused to use an office in the designated capital building, choosing to maintain his state headquarters in a downtown office building. He carried on as much of his business as possible by messenger, refusing to associate with the northerners if at all possible.

Governor Ordway's life was threatened in Yankton so he was glad to go north as quickly as possible. Before the emotional brouhaha simmered down, many political arrangements became known: Governor Ordway's son was confirmed as Territorial auditor, a lucrative position. Jobs in state institutions were handed out to Ordway supporters; many of the assembly legislators arranged to have new counties named after themselves. Lynwood Oyos, an authority on the gubernatorial behavior of territorial and state officials wrote: "Ordway acted boldly in securing passage of the removal bill." He used the customary tactics of jobbery and logrolling to induce voters to approve his wishes.

Other trade-offs and questionable rewards for beneficial services rendered included placement of institutions that the politicians hoped would eventually become state-owned and supported: the territorial university at Vermillion; normal schools at Spearfish, Springfield, and Madison; the reformatory at Plankington, and the Deaf Mute school in Sioux Falls. Governor Ordway scattered promises indiscriminately north and south in return for legislators' voting for the capital removal bill. The penitentiary was first given to Bon Homme, but when the hamlet disappeared, it went to Sioux Falls. Agricultural colleges were promised to both Brookings and Fargo. The northern counties were assigned three normal schools, an insane asylum to Jamestown, and a territorial prison to Bismarck. George Walsh of Grand Forks, a member of the Territorial Council, and unofficial manager of the No. One Hard wheat counties, had supported Bismarck for capital. Grand Forks was promised the University of North Dakota, in expectation of statehood.

Bismarck enjoyed a real estate boom. The newspaper, the *Jamestown Alert* reported: "It is said Aleck McKenzie sold $250,000 worth of land yesterday, and that a half million dollars' worth has changed hands within the last couple days. Most observers then and now thought the selection of Bismarck was foreordained by the Northern Pacific railroad. The railroad furnished the 160-acres of land as required; and Bismarck, just a small town although bigger than some of its competition, eventually raised $100,000 but almost went bankrupt doing so.

The Yankton Oligarchy, especially Attorney General Hugh Campbell, had frequently criticized Governor Ordway and his alleged crimes and misdemeanors. A formal indictment charged Ordway of corrupt practices while in office. He was accused of offering county commissioner offices for sale to the highest bidder, and he was alleged to have accepted a $30,000 bribe for his part in moving the capital from Yankton to Bismarck.

Historical authority Howard Lamar believed that "the conclusion is inescapable that Ordway was one of the most corrupt officials ever to appear in Dakota. He was an excellent example of the cynical post-Civil War politician who brought the political morality of the country to such a low level between 1865 and 1900." Ordway's attorneys moved to quash the indictment on the grounds that a federal employee could not be tried by a territorial court. Chief Justice Alonzo Edgerton, a member of the Yankton Oligarchy, reluctantly granted this motion and Ordway's case was never brought to trial.

Finally, President Chester Arthur succumbed to the storm of letters he received damning Ordway and clamoring for his removal. Ordway also wrote long, eloquent letters to the President and Congress explaining his behavior and denying the charges. President Arthur removed Ordway as Territorial Governor of Dakota Territory on June 25, 1884. He appointed Gilbert Pierce, a Chicago lawyer and playwright, as the new governor.

Ordway, in revengeful fury, sued Hugh Campbell, Attorney General of Dakota Territory, for damaging public statements he had made. The hotheaded and influential Campbell was acquitted, but he was removed from office because of "unbecoming conduct." Ordway settled in Bismarck where he had large real estate holdings and became involved in the management of several banks. He also became a special lobbyist for the Northern Pacific in Washington, thus adding to the belief that he was a willing and dishonest stooge for the railroad and for Alexander McKenzie.

The shift of the capital, followed by the removal of Ordway certainly helped consolidate the thinking of citizens in both north and south in favor of division and statehood. Territorial politics seemed obviously corrupt, and statehood beckoned as the best solution for solving the problems of Dakota Territory.

Cornerstone Laying of New Territorial Capital

The cornerstone laying for the new territorial capital at Bismarck, in September, 1883, was combined with the celebration of the extension of the Northern Pacific railroad into Montana and the driving of the Golden Spike. Four trains with forty-three cars of the Northern Pacific carried Henry Villard, the Northern Pacific president, in addition to a host of famous dignitaries: the former President, General Ulysses Grant; Marshall Field, the Chicago merchant; James J. Hill of the Great Northern Railway; a number of territorial governors, and many foreign personages.

As the long special train rolled through northern Dakota, every hamlet had decorated itself for the visitors. In one spot, two operating threshing machines spewed out grain and straw to dramatize the abundance.

At Bismarck, Alexander McKenzie was in charge of the reception and Governor Ordway (he was not removed until a year later) intro-

The laying of the cornerstone of the capitol building

From the picture collection of the State Historical Society of North Dakota

duced the dignitaries. Throughout the capital city, decorated arches, evergreen branches, banners, and flags created a festive effect. The parade included Sitting Bull carrying a huge American flag, followed by Sioux Indians, one carrying a sign which announced "The March of Civilization."

It had been only seven years since the Custer Massacre – as it was known – which Sitting Bull had been credited with master minding. Through an interpreter Sitting Bull said he was glad to meet the governor and his friends and was inspired by the Great Spirit to shake hands with them (he charged one dollar for his autograph). The crowd gave former President General Grant a standing ovation and insisted that he give a speech, which he reluctantly did. The huge audience was fascinated by Sitting Bull as he sat impassively on the outdoor stage during the long speeches and blew his nose through his fingers.

Huron Convention in 1883 listened to Hugh Campbell

Attorney General Hugh Campbell had suggested that the Huron pre-Constitutional Convention meet in May, 1883, in hopes that the delegates could formulate an approach that would result in statehood.

The March of Civilization

From the picture collection of the State Historical Society of North Dakota

Over four hundred delegates from southern Dakota attended. Many of them were the same people who had attended the Canton convention a year earlier. However, they were no longer so naive as to think statehood could be easily accomplished.

At one point during a debate on the "We Are a State" controversy, Dr. Joseph Ward, speaking about charges of "rebellion" against the United States, said: "Disloyalists usually fight to get out of the Union; we are fighting to get in."

Attorney Campbell insisted that since southern Dakota had fulfilled the traditional requirements for statehood, it was perfectly justified in simply declaring itself an active member of the Union without Congress passing an Enabling Act.

Campbell pointed out that other states had been in this same predicament. For example, Michigan had operated under a functioning state government for fourteen months before it had entered the Union in 1834. Campbell's "We Are a State" concept was based on the belief that the federal government had no power to maintain colonies to be governed at its own pleasure. Campbell claimed that the federal government had no authority to prohibit a territory from becoming a state when it had 60,000 population and fulfilled other requirements. Many agreed with Campbell but feared offending Congress.

Historian Howard Lamar pointed out that "most southern Dakotans were actually more interested in seceding from the Territory and regaining their lost power than they were in becoming a state." However, before the Huron convention adjourned, Campbell's doctrine was incorporated into the convention resolutions, and the group issued a call for a constitutional convention to meet at Sioux Falls, September 5, 1883.

First Sioux Falls Constitutional Convention in 1883

The Sioux Falls convention considered prohibition and women's suffrage and prohibiting cheap sale of public school lands. For reasons of political expediency, the convention decided not to support women's suffrage or prohibition.

However, one of the most important portions of the proposed constitution was General Beadle's school lands clause, in which the future state of South Dakota promised not to sell its school lands for less than ten dollars an acre. The interest on the land sale was to become part of a perpetual fund which would help support the schools. Beadle is honored for "saving the school lands" from profiteers.

Of the 125 delegates, forty-two were lawyers, thirty-one were farmers, thirteen were newspaper editors, eleven were land agents, and the remaining twenty-eight were in a variety of businesses and professions. Only seventeen of the 125 were foreign-born, and the delegates' average age was thirty-five.

The constitution drawn up was similar to those of other states. It was conservative and placed some restriction on taxing and appropriation powers of the legislature and governor, but the clauses proposed for curbing railroads and other big businesses were weak.

Meeting in Fargo about Names for New States

A meeting in Fargo over names for new states—if the time ever came—probably engineered by McKenzie and Ordway, protested southern Dakota's appropriation of the name Dakota in South Dakota and claimed northern Dakota was more entitled to use it because of its production of "Dakota Number One Hard Durum Wheat," famous the world over. Delegates declared that the word "Dakota" was more associated with northern Dakota than with southern. Various names suggested for northern Dakota were Pembina, Algonquin, Chippewa, Ojibway, and Lincoln, which had already been suggested for a Black Hills Territory. Should the two new states be divided North-South across the middle or by the circuitous route of the Missouri River; or on the 46th parallel? Or else where?

First South Dakota Constitution Voted On

Shortly after the first Sioux Falls convention, the proposed constitution came to a vote: 12,336 citizens approved the document and 6814 opposed it, but the shameful fact was that over 30,000 citizens had not cared enough to go to the polls. Congress was unimpressed with the election picture and again rejected statehood, this time because of the lack of popular support.

Sioux Falls Holds Second Constitutional Convention in 1885

Sioux Falls was again the scene of a constitutional convention in 1885. Judge Edgerton again was elected chairman. The delegates made only a few minor changes in the 1883 document. They were mainly concerned with how they could force Congress to award statehood, and how to handle two controversial issues so as not to offend anyone. Gideon Moody, the dominant figure from the Black Hills, cautioned prudence to avoid becoming involved with untried experiments at this crucial time. However, Moody, at the first convention, had announced to the group, "I favor women suffrage.... Give woman the ballot, let her hold office, and you raise her at once in intelligence. I know of no reason why my wife and daughter are not as able to hold office as I am, though they may not be as willing."

Hugh Campbell was back swaying the people with his mesmerizing oratory and scaring the conservatives. Campbell, in his fire-eating speeches, suggested that the people were ready to revolt. Others disagreed and said that most Dakotans were not that concerned about statehood.

Huron's Turn for an Extra-legal Convention

After the Sioux Falls conventions, it was Huron's turn to hold a mock Republican convention in 1885. Huron had won the election to become the temporary capital over Pierre, Sioux Falls, Chamberlain, and others. The dedicated convention-goers nominated Arthur Mellette as governor by acclamation. At the convention of this unborn state, Moody and Edgerton were nominated for the United States Senate, but the nominees did not receive a "secret password" or any instructions on how to break down the door to the Senate. The Democrats ignored the "election" while the Republicans named a full slate of officers.

Dakota citizens voted overwhelmingly in favor of the constitution of 1885. This set the stage if only Congress would relent and pass an Enabling Act to initiate statehood for these determined people and their "squatter legislature."

Hugh Campbell, the old war horse, was deliberately left out of any high office, even a make-believe one. General W. H > H > Beadle, a member of the Yankton Oligarchy, in his *Memoirs* worte this analysis of Campbell's character: "He was a Scotsman—vigorous, persistent, inflexible, and unyielding. Campbell was not admired for kindly and noble qualities but for hsi fighting blood. Always a sledge hammer, he maintained high integrity. He served the cause of division and statehood with great energy but when it became a popular movement, he could not control it."

Although many southern Dakotans admired his fighting spirit, they were afraid of his radicalism and were worried that he would set back the cause of statehood if he openly defied Congress with more of his "We are a State" declarations. Many southern Dakotans were afraid they had already gone too far, that they would never be forgiven and taken into the protective arms of the Union.

In Congress, under Cleveland's Democratic administration, the Butler bill proposed that Dakota Territory be a single state. President Cleveland liked that idea although it did not receive much Congressional support. Dakota disliked the suggestion; the southerners especially yearned to be separated from the northerners. Dakotans shook their heads, wondering why one huge unwieldy state would be preferable to one huge unwieldy territory. Senator Benjamin Harrison of Indiana introduced another statehood bill for two Dakotas but Congress rejected it.

The Oligarchy is Hypocritical

Some of the Yankton Oligarchy—Edgerton, Moody, Kanouse, and Mellette—were still optimistic that deliverance was near and went to Washington to convince President Cleveland that they really did not support Campbell's radical states rights schemes even though it might look that way.

Campbell was furious when he learned of the lack of support of his doctrines when the Oligarchy met President Cleveland. Great was the disappointment over the failure of the Harrison bill to provide two states. The Moody-Edgerton faction and the Campbell faction accused each other of spoiling the chances for the Harrison bill.

In December, like children playing imaginary games, the unofficial state legislature met in Huron for another attempt at make-believe. Campbell was down-hearted because Mellette was too cautious to enact laws and defy the federal government by activating a "squatter" legislature. Many so-called legislators became disheartened and went home early. Soon no quorum was present and the legislature adjourned. Before it disbanded, the group held a reception and dance at the Grand, a brilliant affair with the elaborate decorations in honor of the first assemblage of the "Dakota State Legislature," but the politicians and their wives were hard put to come up with a reason for celebration; the couples danced mechanically and they smiled with false optimism about the future, deciding they derived no pleasure from pretending to be something they were not—an official state.

Disappointments Pile Up

The disappointments accumulated. The Yankton statehood forces decided they should enlist the help of northern Dakota instead of ignoring it. Hugh Campbell, who was so often used and abused, worked hard to direct a complete campaign throughout Dakota to stimulate interest in statehood. The vote on the division question in November, 1887, gave the statehood leaders a stunning shock. Northern Dakota voted 18,000 to 8,000 against division. In southern Dakota the vote was 15,000 to 14,000 against division. These results were blamed on the powerful influences of the Northern Pacific railroad and the incumbent Democrats.

Nothing Worked

Single-state advocates were encouraged and held a convention of their own at Aberdeen to oppose division and to back the Butler bill for one state. With all the ups and downs, the discouraged leaders hardly knew what to do. But because of the dissension and the increasing discussions of the issues, the people became more involved in what was going on among the politicians.

It seemed that no matter what the politicians and the people tried, nothing worked. Campbell exhausted himself speaking to conventions and village meetings where the audience enjoyed his pyrotechnics even if they didn't always understand his logic for his "We Are a State" proposals.

The division and statehood convention met in City Hall at Huron on July 10, 1888, and was called to order by Campbell. In addition to urging the people to work for division and statehood, he quoted a favorite bit of verse: "What consititutes a state? Men! High-minded men. Men, who their duties know, but know their rights, and knowing, dare maintain. These constitute a State. Let us be men who know our rights."

This era was the highlight of his political career, and the average person began to believe his questionable but persuasive proposals to Congress and pretending to be a legitimate state as the only way to achieve statehood.

Victory at Last

In 1888, it took a national election to guarantee statehood for both Dakotas. Benjamin Harrison of Indiana, Mellette's old friend, won the election to be the next President of the United States; he was the

Republican senator who had introduced a bill for statehood for both
Dakotas. And now he would soon
be President. Congress began to
give some serious consideration to
the territories pounding at the gates
of the Union; two Dakotas, Montana, and Washington were slated
to come in as states. The Senate
balance would be maintained by an
even number of Democratic and
Republican senators who would
come into the fold, and other political problems were straightened out
to the satisfaction of both parties.

Benjamin Harrison

*From the picture collection of the State
Historical Society of North Dakota*

Historian Kingsbury reported on
the celebrations over the
Republican victories; if there was
an entertainment Dakotans reveled
in, it was a celebration for a happy
event like a Republican victory. Yanktonians celebrated with a mammoth parade complete with a coronet band, a fife and drum corps,
fireworks, the din of gun-powder explosions, drinking noisy toasts, the
boisterous exchange of congratulations and optimistic predictions for
the future. Numerous huge transparencies were scattered throughout
the procession; one sketch presented an unmistakable jackass in the
act of hurling Cleveland from the saddle. Underneath was a farewell:
"Good-bye Grover!"

Kingsbury summed up the excitement: "It was a carnival of exulta-
tion which spent itself only when the forces were exhausted.... As the
cavalcade slowly unwound itself the brilliancy of the display evoked
the wildest enthusiasm from a multitude of people of all ages, both
sexes, waving flags, handkerchiefs, or uplifted hands.... There was a
half mile of moving column ablaze with torches, fireworks, colored
lights and transparencies, wending its way between two walls of il-

lumination and under a canopy of flame and sparks and smoke from burning fireworks."

President Cleveland Signs the Enabling Act

At last, President Grover Cleveland, ten days before his term ended, signed the Enabling Act (also called the Omnibus Bill) on Washington's birthday, February 22, 1889, authorizing the creation of constitutions in North Dakota, South Dakota, Montana, and Washington. The President used a pen made from the quill of an eagle killed in Dakota Territory. Fortunately, whether the historic pen came from northern or southern Dakota was not revealed. Jubilation reigned in Congress. Senators and Congressmen threw books and papers into the air and pounded each other on the back, even though they were political enemies. Nothing could stop official Statehood now.

Although tired after waiting so many years, people in the Dakotas still had energy to celebrate, exchange congratulations, and shake hands until they ached. Huge bonfires blazed from Yankton to Bismarck, from the Black Hills to the Red River Valley and all the settlements in between. The electrifying news "We are a State" hopped, skipped and jumped up and down every curve and loop of the Missouri River in North Dakota and in South Dakota.

Southern Dakota Holds Third Constitutional Convention in Sioux Falls

Southern Dakota delegates convened for their third Constitutional Convention in Sioux Falls in July, 1889. Actually, there wasn't much to do. The delegates approved the Constitution they had first written in 1883 and approved the revision they had made in 1885. They worked to conform to the rules and regulations for entering the Union as required by the Enabling Act. The seasoned politicians noticed there were some new types of delegates at the convention, not politicians but informed farmers who belonged to the new Farmer's Alliance.

They had come to the convention to present their own ideas about statehood, agricultural problems, and railroads, and how to prevent the Yankton Ring from controlling all the decisions.

Northern Dakota Holds First Constitutional Convention in Bismarck

Northern Dakota delegates met in Bismarck for their Constitutional extravaganza on July 4, 1889, with a colorful parade commemorating their march into statehood. There was never a North Dakota flag-waving parade so spectacular before or since. Entertaining the crowds were cavalry and a band from Fort Yates, cavalry from Fort Lincoln, the Valley City band, members of the newly-organized press association, pretty girls on horseback representing the thirty-eight states and the four new ones, plus delegates to the Constitutional Convention.

Constitutional Parade held July 4, 1889

From the picture collection of the State Historical Society of North Dakota

As if protecting the rear of the parade from ambush, five hundred Sioux attired in dazzling regalia and wearing iridescent feathered war bonnets, glided by on foot or pranced on their horses up the street, led by Sitting Bull who wore a black Prince Albert frock coat. Rain-in-the-Face, who, according to one of the many legends of the Custer Massacre, had cut out Tom Custer's heart then eaten it, rode his spirited horse with an American flag draped over one ear and an Irish emblem over the horse's other ear.

Historic Convention Begins

Frederick Fancher

From the picture collection of the State Historical Society of North Dakota

The next day, the work of this first northern Dakota Constitutional Convention began. The delegates, mostly young men, elected Fred Fancher of Jamestown president of the Convention. He was a leader of the powerful Dakota Farmer's Alliance. Mr. Fancher addressed the delegates: "I hardly know how to find words in which to express my thanks for the honor you have conferred on me, in selecting me the president of this magnificent convention.... I am not very well versed in parliamentary rules but I think I will venture to promise to do my best to please you."

Henry Blackwell of Boston, Secretary of the Women Suffrage association of the United States, addressed the assemblage. He said; "We have been urging this moment for fifty years.... We argue that it is right under the Declaration of Independence for women to be voters. The highest argument in their favor is that women are law-abiding citizens.... When we have organized on these Great Plains the leading communities of America, we call that all exclaim with Longfellow in his apostrophe to the Union: 'Thou too, sail on, O Ship of State!' "

The delegates argued about prohibition. Mr. Rowe of Dickey County said: "When we come into statehood, we wish to come over the threshold with an article in our Constitution that is in favor of free homes, free speech, and a free press, and against the freedom of the rum power."

After several others had spoken pro and con about Prohibition, Mr. O'Brien of Ramsey County commented: "I don't see what good it would do for us to say here in this constitution that any man who gets drunk two or three times a week should be removed from office, and it is left so that Legislature can fix the number of times that man must get drunk to constitute habitual drunkenness."

Other individual contributions by delegates dealt with a variety of subjects.

Mr. Robertson of Walsh County was a grammarian and explained how to use who, whom and which.

Mr. Rolfe of Benson County responded: "It strikes me that the question is: what is the antecedent of the pronoun?"

Mr. Blewett of Stutsman County made a motion: "I move that the speeches be limited to three minutes." The motion was seconded and adopted.

Mr. Turner of Bottineau County made a motion: "I saw plainly that the interests of the State of North Dakota would be sold by the people of Bismarck for the purpose of establishing the capital here.... The position of things was such that I could not vote for the City of Bismarck without voting for the location of the other institutions which I am opposed to locating. For that reason, I record my vote NO...."

Mr. Spalding of Cass County said: "I have sat here and listened to gas and buncome and demagoguery on all sides, on what was supposed to be on behalf of the poor man. But I would like to know what this fund is for. What are we getting up a constitution for?"

John Wesley Powell, Director of the Geological Survey and head of the Smithsonian Bureau of Ethnology, had been invited to speak to the delegates: "I am not accustomed to speak on occasions like this.... I have made some study, and in my remarks I will confine myself wholly to some practical questions relating to irrigation. The state of North Dakota has a curious position geographically in relation to agricultural purposes: the western part has insufficient rainfall and the western portion is, practically, wholly dependent on irrigation. In the western portion, all dependence on rains will ultimately bring disaster to the people.... Don't let these streams get out of the possession of the people. If you fail in making a Constitution in any other respect, fail NOT in this one. Take lessons from California and Colorado. Fix it in your constitution that no corporation—no body of men—nor capital can get possession and right to your waters. Hold the waters in the hands of the people."

John Wesley Powell

From the picture collection of the State Historical Society of North Dakota

Arthur Mellette, the popular governor of Dakota Territory, had been invited to speak to the convention. He said: "One of the greatest evils is excessive legislation, the constant change every two years of the laws, and the squabbles and debates over the different questions that constantly arise. It is wise, in my judgment, after the people have decided in which direction their interests lie, to embody them in a fundamental law of the land and make it permanent."

Copies of the constitution of other states were available to the delegates. The constitution proposed for South Dakota was on the desk of each member; thus the experience of other states was freely drawn upon.

As might have been expected, the Northern Pacific Railroad had suggestions for the North Dakota constitution. Henry Villard, the chairman of the Northern Pacific board, had requested Professor James Thayer of Harvard Law School to write a proposed constitution for North Dakota. According to historical expert Elwyn Robinson, it was "a carefully constructed model constitution, not a dishonest effort to create a government favorable to the railroads." The Thayer version was introduced by delegate Martin Williams of Bismarck who refused to reveal who wrote it. This reticence caused much speculation.

The constitution that was finally adopted used much of Thayer's phrasing. Yet it embodied the radical, progressive spirit of North Dakota. The people of northern Dakota believed they had always been exploited by railroads as well as by the grain monopolies of Minneapolis and they wished to legislate against them.

The hard-working delegates considered every measure that was considered radical and popular at the time: minority representation, the initiative, referendum, and recall. The group eventually worked out a liberal legislative program of reform. The document did place a number of limitations on the powers of the governor and the legislature.

Many acrimonious debates were held on almost every proposal, but the two issues that caused the most fights were where the state institutions should be established and how to control the railroads and other big business. The recommendation about the state holding onto water rights, suggested by John Wesley Powell, was included in the Constitution. General Beadle's protective clause to prevent school lands from being sold for less than ten dollars an acre was incorporated. Women's suffrage and prohibition did not pass.

Governor Mellette's advice about writing specific laws to avoid frequent revision was followed. A long constitution was the result, six times as long as the federal constitution. The voters ratified the constitution 27,441 to 8,107. The dissenters were believed to be citizens who did not think the new state should start with fourteen institutions or who did not approve of their chosen locations. Public institutions were located by constitution but were seldom funded until much later.

Joint Commission of North Dakota and South Dakota

A feature of the North Dakota Constitutional Convention in 1889 was that the two Dakotas were the only pair of states created from one territory which achieved statehood simultaneously. The Enabling Act required that the two conventions should appoint a Joint Commission to meet at Bismarck to agree upon a division of property, the disposition of the territorial library and public records, and the adjustment of territorial debts. The twin states, as they were often called, certainly were not identical and often did not feel at all fraternal, but these often incompatible twins were instructed to reach an amicable agreement on many dilemmas.

Each state appointed seven delegates who met for three weeks during the Constitutional Convention in Bismarck to divide the common property and balance territorial accounts. To balance the account for what Dakota Territory had paid to establish institutions, South Dakota, with ten institutions, had to pay $22,085.35 to North Dakota, which had only four institutions.

Decisions had to be made about guns, arms, camp equipment for soldiers, table ware, and kitchen utensils. Dr. Valentine McGillycuddy, a member of the South Dakota commission and the noted former Indian Agent at Pine Ridge Reservation, SD, discovered 844 rifles stored in the capitol. They were counted out equitably.

After the committee work was completed in a congenial atmosphere, the South Dakota Chairman, Judge A. G. Kellam, made the following closing comments: "On behalf of the Joint Commission of South Dakota, I want to say to you Gentlemen of the North, from whom we are about to separate that, did we not live in a land where every women is a queen and every man a king, and did we possess the power, I would be glad to place a coronet upon the brow of every citizen of the empire state of North Dakota." (*CHEERS*)

When North Dakota achieved statehood, Bismarck became the temporary capital. Schemes for locating the permanent capital engrossed the attention of the Constitutional Convention immediately. Bismarck had two strong competitors: Grand Forks in Grand Forks County and Jamestown in Stutsman County. There were debates, speeches, trade-off deals, indignation meetings, and caucuses. An obstreperous member of the committee shouted out from the gallery "*Rats!*" Another responded by yelling an unprintable oath. At last the Stutsman County delegation decided it was in its best interests and also best for the new state to cast their votes for Bismarck. Others soon followed their lead. Delegate Stevens, in explaining his vote said: "I voted aye on this proposition so that the City of Bismarck may sit on her seven hills, and be the most beautiful capital of the four new states."

North Dakotans elected John Miller as their first governor. Miller was the manager of a Bonanza Farm in the Red River Valley which operated 27,000 acres. He was against the new state becoming involved in the Louisiana Lottery and was for Prohibition. I. R. Casey of Jamestown and Gilbert A. Pierce, former governor of Dakota Territory, were elected United States Senators.

South Dakota honored Territorial Governor Arthur Mellette by electing him as its first governor. The Sioux Falls Constitution, which had been almost ready for use since 1883, was approved unanimously.

John Miller, first governor of North Dakota

From the picture collection of the State Historical Society of North Dakota

Gideon Moody, a conservative politician and Civil War hero from Deadwood, and Richard Pettigrew, a hard-working booster for Sioux Falls, were elected as South Dakota's United States Senators. General W.H.H. Beadle, called "the patron saint of the schools," became president of the State Normal School at Madison, SD. Territorial Judge Alonzo Edgerton became judge of the Circuit Court.

Of the Yankton Oligarchy only the firebrand Hugh Campbell was not awarded high office for his tireless but controversial work for statehood. Some historians hailed him as "the wheel horse" of the movement, but he never realized his ambition to become a U.S. Senator.

At the third constitutional convention at Sioux Falls in the summer of 1889, the delegates voted to establish a temporary capital of South Dakota. Competing for this honor were Chamberlain, Huron, Mitchell, Redfield, Sioux Falls, Watertown, and Pierre. Each hopeful contender organized publicity and

Richard Pettigrew, first South Dakota Senator

From the picture collection of the State Historical Society of North Dakota

propaganda groups and collected money through subscription or issued municipal bonds and warrants. The excitement and interest generated by the capital contest commanded the attention of the citizens, much more so than did the constitution. According to an unidentified author in the *South Dakota Historical Collections* (who may be South Dakota historian Doane Robinson), the dishonest campaigns were "wholesale corruption of voters; and from the standpoint of morals, it was a most unhappy time."

Pierre won the election receiving 27,096 votes with Huron coming in second with 14,914. In triumphant Pierre, the House met in the court house, and the Senate in the GAR building. The citizens went to work immediately to construct a temporary capitol building, and it was ready for use when the legislature met on January 1, 1890. The land was donated by the Chicago and Northwestern Railroad, and the enthusiastic boosters donated cash.

According to the Constitution, the permanent capital had to be voted on in the fall of 1890. Pierre was again victorious over Huron. *The South Dakota Collections* author wrote: "Both cities bankrupted themselves to prosecute the fight, and it is another campaign over which it is perhaps charitable to throw the mantle of obscurity."

Despite continuous fighting for years — even into the 20th century — over removing the permanent state capital to another city, PEERLESS PIERRE maintained its title, the state capital of South Dakota.

Reverend Joseph Ward, the most beloved figure in the Yankton Oligarchy and the Statehood Movement, died nine days after statehood became official. Many relatives and friends crowded tear-

First South Dakota capitol at Pierre

Photograph courtesy State Historical Society of South Dakota

fully around his bedside to bid him farewell. He died at age fifty-one of a carbuncle. Among Reverend Ward's outstanding and lasting contributions to the new state he did not live to enjoy was the South Dakota state motto: "Under God the people rule." The motto reflects Dr. Ward's philosophy of government.

Captain John Blair Smith Todd, who had been so influential in the early days of Dakota Territory, died in 1872 at Yankton, age fifty-eight, before the Statehood Movement began.

Chief Strike-the-Ree, who had been consistently loyal and courageous in his devotion to encouraging peace and accord between the Yanktons and whites no matter what happened, died one year before Statehood, in 1888, at age eighty-four or ninety-four. At his request, he was buried with medallions from three Presidents of the United States, bearing likenesses of the donors: the first from Thomas Jefferson given to his father by Lewis and Clark; the second from James Buchanan; and the third from Ulysses Grant. Old Strike was one of the most honored and respected Indians in the entire United States. Historian Doane Robinson said: "Strike-the-Ree was an extraordinary man, possessing honesty and excellent judgment. He adhered to the provisions of the Treaty of 1858 with a fidelity which amounted to a religious zeal."

Sitting Bull, the Hunkpapa Sioux, whose last days were spent at Standing Rock Reservation (half in northern Dakota and half in southern Dakota) died in 1890 at age fifty-nine, a year after Statehood. Sitting Bull's body, which was first buried at Fort Yates in North Dakota, was later spirited away by South Dakotans. His grave is now located near Mobridge, SD.

Agent James McLaughlin at Standing Rock was worried because Sitting Bull was a leader in the Ghost Dance craze and new Messiah religion practiced by many Sioux. He insisted that he feared an uprising. McLaughlin gave orders for Sitting Bull's arrest and "under no circumstances to let him escape." While resisting arrest, Sitting Bull was shot by the Indian police. His killing occurred several weeks before the tragic Battle of Wounded Knee, also known as the Messiah War.

Sitting Bull had more influence than any other medicine man/chief in uniting the many tribes of the Northern Plains in a stubborn campaign of resistance to the whites and their demands for land. Sitting Bull refused to touch a pen to the white man's treaties. Whether people considered Sitting Bull a civilized devil or an uncivilized god, they were always fascinated with his commanding personality and appearance.

Sitting Bull

From the picture collection of the State Historical Society of North Dakota

Modern white scholars of Indian history, Herbert T. Hoover and Robert C. Hollow, in *The Last Years of Sitting Bull*, have summed up his significance: "Sitting Bull earned fame among followers, public officials, occasional visitors, and an international body of admirers as a successful soldier, an astute diplomat, a resourceful field marshal for inter-tribal forces, an eminent medicine man, a symbol of resistance, and a curator of Indian traditions. For all these reasons his name is etched boldly in the annals of North America."

Official Statehood at Last

The new president, Republican Benjamin Harrison, signed the document admitting North and South Dakota to the Union on November 2, 1889. He tactfully shuffled the two proclamations in such a way that observers could not tell which was signed first.

"They were born together; they are one, and I will make them twins," announced President Harrison. Based on alphabetical order, North Dakota is the thirty-ninth state and South Dakota the fortieth.'

The *Sioux Falls Argus-Leader* ran a banner headline: UNCLE SAM'S NEW TWINS. Happy citizens throughout the two states celebrated official statehood, but it was anti-climactic after the passage of the Enabling Act. Still, Dakotans everywhere were always willing to celebrate one more time and thank the Lord for the long-awaited victory.

In 1889, the Statehood Year, The United States government, with the urging of Richard Pettigrew, the new United States Senator from Sioux Falls, paid $25,000 to purchase, deliver, and install 720 quartizte markers weighing 800 pounds each along the entire border between North and South Dakota. On one side of each marker on its 10-inch square sides is chiseled "N.D."; "S.D." on the other; and "M" on a third side for mileage from the initial east marker. Most of these century-old markers are still in place. The Two Dakotas are the only states in the Union to be so markeed, according to Gordon Iseminger, a history professor at the University of North Dakota.

The *Bismarck Tribune*, November 3, 1889, published the following verse with an illustration of a smiling Uncle Sam pointing to a large map of North Dakota and South Dakota, divided at last on the seventh standard parallel.

THE BIRTH OF THE TWINS

Good morn', Uncle Samuel, proudly we meet you.
And throw with our finger-tips, kisses galore.
We're not very old, but with sunshine we greet you.
And ask but your blessing—no less and no more.

We've heard of you, Uncle, in truth we learned to love you.
We've longed for this union where greatness begins.
And now with our babyhood banners above you
We pledge you the lives of these turbulent twins.

The *Yankton Daily Press and Dakotan*, November 2, 1889, published a series of one column headlines:

WE ARE A STATE

The Proclamation Issued for
South and North Dakota

Two New Stars Shining from the
Firmament of the Union

Ring the bells and Shoot the
Cannon—E. Pluribus Unum

A Brief Announcement of the
Glorious News, But it is Enough

Bibliography

Books

Andreas, A. T. *Andreas' Historical Atlas of Dakota*. (Chicago: Donnelly & Sons, 1884).

Andrist, Ralph K. *To The Pacific with Lewis and Clark*. (New York: American Heritage Publishing Company, 1947).

Armstrong, Moses K. *The Early Empire Builders of the Great West* (St. Paul: E. W. Porter, 1901).

Athearn, Robert G. *Forts of the Upper Missouri* (Lincoln: University of Nebraska Press, 1967).

Bennett, Estelline. *Old Deadwood Days*. (New York: Charles Scribner's Sons, 1935).

Berg, Franci M. *North Dakota . . Land of Changing Seasons*. (Hettinger, ND: Flying Diamond Books—Printed by North Plains Press, Aberdeen, South Dakota, 1977).

Bradley, Van Allen. *The New Gold in Your Attic*. (New York: Fleet Press Corporation, 1958).

Briggs, Harold E. *Frontiers of the Northwest: A History of the Upper Missouri Valley*. (New York: D. Appleton-Century Company, 1940).

Brooks, Chester L. and Mattison, Ray H. *Theodore Roosevelt and the Dakota Badlands*. (Washington, DC: National Park Service, 1958).

Brown, Dee. *Bury My Heart at Wounded Knee*. (New York: Holt, Rinehart & Winston, 1971).

Brown, Jess, and Willard, A. M. *The Black Hills Trails*. (Rapid City: Rapid City Journal Company, 1924).

Carley, Kenneth. *The Sioux Uprising of 1862.* (St Paul: The Minnesota Historical Society, 1961).

Casey, Robert J. *The Black Hills and Their Incredible Characters.* (New York: The Bobbs-Merrill Company, 1949).

Catlin, George. *Letters and Notes on the North American Indians.* (New York: Clarkston N. Potter, Inc., 1975).

Chittenden, Hiram Martin. *A History of the American Fur Trade of the Far West.* (Stanford, California: Adademic Reprints, vol. 1, 1954).

Coursey, O. W. *Pioneering in Dakota.* (Mitchell, South Dakota: Educator Supply Company, 1937).

Custer, Elizabeth B. *Boots and Saddles.* (Norman: University of Oklahoma Press, 1961).

Cwach, Elmer D. *A History of the Yankton Indian Agency During the Nineteenth Century.* (Vermillion: University of South Dakota, 1958).

Dalton, John Elmer. *A History of the Location of the State Capital in South Dakota.* (Vermillion: The Governmental Research Bureau, University of South Dakota, 1945).

DeWall, Robb. *The Saga of Sitting Bull's Bones.* (Crazy Horse, South Dakota: Korczak's Heritage, 1984).

Dick, Everett. *The Sod House Frontier A Social History of the Northern Plains from the Creation of Kansas and Nebraska to the Admission of the Dakotas.* (New York: D. Appleton-Century Company Inc., 1937).

Dick, Everett. *Vanguards of the Frontier A Social History of the Northern Plains and Rocky Mountains from the Fur Traders to the Sod Busters.* (Lincoln: University of Nebraska Press, 1941).

Eastman, Elaine Goodale, 1885-1891. *Sister to the Sioux.* (Lincoln: University of Nebraska Press, 1978).

Federal Writers' Project. *North Dakota: A Guide to the Northern*

Prairie State. (New York: Oxford University Press, 1938; second edition, 1950).

Federal Writers Project. *A South Dakota Guide.* (Sponsored by the State of South Dakota, 1938).

Fischer, Christiane, ed. *Women in the American West Let Them Speak for Themselves.* (New York: E. P. Dutton, 1978).

Fish, Herbert Clay and Black, R. M. *A Brief History of North Dakota.* (New York: American Book Company, 1925).

Friggens, Paul. *Gold and Grass The Black Hills Story.* (Boulder, Colorado: Pruett Publishing Company, 1983).

Garraty, John A. *Theodore Roosevelt – The Strenuous Life.* (New York: American Heritage Publishing Company, 1967).

Gilmore, Melvin Randolph. *Prairie Smoke A Collection of Lore of the Prairies.* (Bismarck: Bismarck Tribune Print, 1921).

Graham, W. A. (ed.) *The Custer Myth.* (Harrisburg, Pennsylvania: Bonanza Books, The Telegraph Press, 1953).

Hagedorn, Herman. (ed.) *The Theodore Roosevelt Treasury – A Self-Portait from His Writings.* (New York: G. P. Putnam's Sons, 1957).

Hall, Bert L. *Roundup Years, Old Muddy to Black Hills.* (Pierre, South Dakota: The Reminder, Inc., 1956).

Hanson, Nancy Edmonds. *'Cross the Wide Missouri* The Missouri River and Lake Sakakawea. Vol. 1, North Dakota Centennial Series. (Fargo, North Dakota: The Dakota Graphic Society, 1984).

Holley, Frances Chamberlain. *Once Their Home or Our Legacy from the Dakotahs.* (Chicago: Donahue & Henneberry, 1892).

Hollow, Robert C. and Hoover, Herbert T. *The Last Years of Sitting Bull.* (Bismarck, North Dakota: Museum Division, State Historical Society of North Dakota, 1984).

Hoover, Herbert T. (ed.) *Planning for the South Dakota Centennial: A Bibliography.* (University of South Dakota, Vermillion:

University of South Dakota Committee on the Humanities, 1984).

Hughes, Richard B. *Pioneer Years in the Black Hills.* (Glendale, California: Arthur H. Clark Company, 1957).

Hunt, Jane. (ed.) *Brevet's South Dakota Historical Markers.* (Sioux Falls, South Dakota: Brevet Press, a division of Brevet International, Inc., 1974).

Jackson, Donald. *Custer's Gold.* (Lincoln: University of Nebraska Press by Yale University, 1966).

Jackson, Helen Hunt. *Century of Dishonor.* (Minneapolis: Ross and Haines, Inc., 1964).

Jennewein, J. Leonard and Boorman, Jane, (editors). *Dakota Panorama.* (Sioux Falls, South Dakota: Dakota Territory Centennial Commission, Midwest-Beach Printing Company, 1962).

Karolevitz, Robert F. *Challenge—The South Dakota Story.* (Sioux Falls: Brevet Press, Inc., 1975).

Karolevitz, Robert F. *Yankton: A Pioneer Past.* (Aberdeen: North Plains Press, 1972).

Kingsbury, George W. *History of Dakota Territory.* 5 vols. (Chicago: S. J. Clark Company, 1915).

Krause, Herbert and Olson, Gary D. *Custer's Prelude to Glory.* (Sioux Falls: Brevet Press, 1974).

Lamar, Howard. *Dakota Territory 1861-1889.* (New Haven: Yale University Press, 1956).

LaPointe, James. *Legends of the Lakota.* (San Francisco: The Indian Historian Press, 1976).

Lass, William E. *A History of Steamboating on the Upper Missouri River.* (Lincoln: University of Nebraska Press, 1962).

Lee, Bob and Williams, Dick. *Last Grass Frontier: The South Dakota Stock Grower Heritage.* (Sturgis, South Dakota: Black Hills Publications, Inc., 1964).

Lee, Bob (ed.) *Gold-Gals-Guns-Guts*. (Deadwood-Lead: '76 Centennial Inc., 1976).

Lounsberry, Clement C. *North Dakota History and People*. 3 vols. (Chicago: S. J. Clarke Publishing Company, 1917).

McGillycuddy, Julia. *McGillycuddy—Agent*. (Stanford: Stanford University Press, 1941).

McLaughlin, James. *My Friend the Indian*. (Boston & New York: Houghton-Mifflin, Riverside Press, Cambridge, 1910).

Meyer, Roy W. *The Village Indians of the Upper Missouri*. (Lincoln: University of Nebraska Press, 1977).

Milton, John R. *South Dakota-A Bicentennial History*. (New York: W. W. Norton & Company, Inc. and Nashville: American Association for State and Local History, 1977).

Myres, Sandra L. *Westering Women and the Frontier Experience, 1800-1915*. (Albuquerque: University of New Mexico, 1982).

Nelson, Bruce. *Land of the Dacotahs*. (Minneapolis: University of Minnesota Press, 1946).

Official Report of the Proceedings and Debates of the First Constitutional Convention of North Dakota. Assembled in the city of Bismarck, July 4th to August 17th, 1889. R. M. Tuttle, Official Stenographer. (Bismarck, North Dakota: Bismarck Tribune State Printers and Binders, 1889).

Olson, James C. *Red Cloud and the Sioux Problem*. (Lincoln: University of Nebraska Press, 1965).

Oyos, Lynwood E. *Over a Century of Leadership—South Dakota Territorial and State Governors 1861-1987 — A Retrospective*. (Sioux Falls: Department of History, Augustana College, Center for Western Studies: Crescent Publishing, Hills, Minnesota, 1987).

Parker, Watson. *Deadwood—The Golden Years*. (Lincoln: University of Nebraska Press, 1981).

Parker, Watson. *Gold in the Black Hills.* (Lincoln: University of Nebraska Press, Bison edition, 1982).

Piper, Marion J. *Dakota Portraits.* (Bismarck: Dakota Territory Centennial Commission, 1964).

Powell, John Wesley, Director. *Fourth Annual Report of Bureau of Ethnology to the Secretary of the Smithsonian Institute, 1882-1883.* (Washington, D.C.: Government Printing Office, 1886).

Rezatto, Helen. *Mount Moriah "Kill a man—Start a Cemetery."* *(Aberdeen: North Plains Press, 1980).*

Rezatto, Helen. *Tales of the Black Hills.* (Aberdeen: North Plains Press, 1983).

Robinson, Doane, (ed.). *Constitutional Debates.* Dakota Constitutional Convention Held at Sioux Falls, September, 1885 — Vol. 1.

Robinson, Doane, (ed). *A Brief History of South Dakota.* (New York: American Book Company, 1905).

Robinson, Doane, (ed.). *History of South Dakota* Vol 1. Aberdeen: B. F. Brown & Company, 1901).

Robinson, Doane. *A History of the Dakota or Sioux Indians.* (Minneapolis: Ross & Haines, 1904).

Robinson, Elwyn B. *History of North Dakota.* (Lincoln: University of Nebraska Press, 1966).

Rolfsrud, Erling. *Lanterns Over the Prairie.* (Brainerd, Minnesota: Lakeland Color Press, Brainerd, Minnesota, 1949).

Rolfsrud, Erling. *The Story of North Dakota.* (Alexandria, Minnesota: Lantern Books, 1963).

Sansom-Flood, Renee. *Lessons from Chouteau Creek* Yankton Memories of Territorial Intrigue. Dakota Series—Number 1. (Sioux Falls, South Dakota: Augustana College, Center for Western Studies. Printed by Crescent Publishing Inc., Hills Minnesota, 1986).

Sansom-Flood, Renee and Bernie, Shirley A. *Remember Your Rela-*

tives. Yankton Sioux Images, 1851 to 1904. (Marty, South Dakota: Marty Indian School, 1985).

Saum, Lewis O. *The Fur Trader and the Indian.* (Seattle: University of Washington Press, 1965).

Schell, Herbert S. *History of South Dakota,* third edition. (Lincoln, University of Nebraska Press, 1975).

Schulenberg, Raymond F. *Indians of North Dakota.* (Bismarck: State Historical Society of North Dakota, 1956).

Seymour, Flora Warren. *Indian Agents of the Old Frontier.* (New York: D. Appleton-Century Company, 1941).

Slaughter, Linda W. Mrs. *The New Northwest.* A Pamphlet stating Briefly the Advantages of Bismarck and Vicinity, Soil, Timber, Climate, Settlements, Business, etc. (Bismarck: Bismarck Tribune Print, 1874) Published by Burleigh County Pioneers Association.

Slaughter, Linda W. *Fortress to Farm* or Twenty-Three years on the frontier. (ed). Hazel Eastman. (New York: An Exposition-Lochinvar Book, Exposition Press, 1972).

Sneve, Virginia Driving Hawk. *The Dakotas' Heritage.* (Webster, South Dakota: Reporter and Farmer, 1973).

South Dakota Historical Collections. Vols. 2, 4, 5, 12, 16. (Aberdeen: News Printing Company, 1904, 1912).

Stevens, James. *Paul Bunyan.* (Garden City, New York: Garden City Publishing Company by Alfred A. Knopf, 1925).

Stewart, Edgar I. *Custer's Luck.* (Norman: The Macmillan Company, 1930).

Tallent, Annie D. *The Black Hills or the Last Hunting Grounds of the Dakotahs.* Second Edition. (Sioux Falls: Brevet Press, 1974).

Thwaites, Reuben Gold, (ed.) *Original Journals of the Lewis and Clark Expedition,* 1804-1806. Vol. 1 (New York: Arno Press, a Publishing and Literary Service of the New York Times, 1896).

Van Nuys, Laura Bower. *The Family Band* — From the Missouri to the Black Hills, 1881-1900. (Lincoln: University of Nebraska Press, 1967).

Waldo, Edna LaMoore. *Dakota.* Caldwell, Idaho: Caxton Printers, 1936).

Webb, Walter Prescott. *The Great Plains.* (New York: Grosset and Dunlap, 1931).

Wemett, William Marks. *The Story of the Flickertail State.* (Valley City, North Dakota: W. M. Wemett, 1923).

Whitman, Wanda, (ed.) *Songs That Changed the World.* (New York: Crown Publishers, 1969).

Wyman, Walker D. Frontier Woman. *The Life of a Woman Homesteader on the Dakota Frontier.* (Grace Fairchild) (River Falls, Wisconsin: University of Wisconsin Press, River Falls Press, 1972).

Journals and Articles

Beadle, W. H. H. "Beadle's Memoirs," *South Dakota Historical Collections,* Vol. V (1906), 174-220

Beadle, W. H. H. "Removal of the Capital to Bismarck," *South Dakota Historical Collections,* Vol. V (1910), 131-135.

Black, R. M. "History of the State Constitutional Convention of 1889," *North Dakota Historical Collections*, Vol. II (1910), 111-157.

Boller, Henry A. "Journal of a Trip To, and Residence In, the Indian Country," *North Dakota History*, Vol. 33, no. 3 (Summer, 1966).

Fleetwood, Mary. "Dakota's First Historian: Moses K. Armstrong, 1832-1906," *North Dakota History*, Vol.37, No. 3 (Summer, 1970).

Foster, James S. "Outlines of History of Territory of Dakota and Emigrants' Guide," *South Dakota Historical Collections*, Vol. XII, 71-178.

French, Kathryn M. "Manuel Lisa," *South Dakota Historical Collections.* Vol. XII, 71-78.

Green, Caroll Gardner. "The Struggle of South Dakota to Become a State," *Collections of the State Historical Society of South Dakota,* Vol. 13, (1924).

Green, Charles Lowell. "The Indian Reservation System of the Dakotas to 1889," *South Dakota Historical Collections,* Vol XIV, (1928) 100-120.

Miller, John, "First Message of the Governor of North Dakota to the Legislative Assembly, Delivered at Bismarck, November 20, 1889," *North Dakota History,* Vol 31, No. 3 (July, 1964) 167-187.

Peterson, Susan, "From Paradise to Prairie: The Presentation Sisters in Dakota, 1880-1896. *South Dakota History,* Vol 10, No. 3 (Summer, 1980) 210-222.

Robinson, Doane. "Fort Manuel," *Department of History Collections.* Vol. XII (1924) 99-122.

Robinson, Elwyn B., "The Themes of North Dakota History," (This article is a revision of an address read on November 6, 1958, at the Seventy-Fifth Anniversary Conference of the University of North Dakota, Grand Forks).

Robinson, Will G. "Our Indian Problems," South Dakota Historical Collections, Vol. XXV (1951), 350-360.

Spalding, Burleigh F. "Constitutional Convention, 1889," *North Dakota History.* Vol. 31, No. 3 (July, 1964), 151-164.

Vossler, Bill, "Quartzite Pillars Divide Dakotas," *Centennial Sentinel.* Vol. 2, No. 3 (August/September, 1988).

Wheelock, Ralph W. "The Tour of the Capital Commission," and "Capitol Commission Correspondence," *South Dakota Historical Collections.* Vol. V. (1910), 140-171.

Wilson, Wesley C. "Doctor Walter A. Burleigh: Dakota Territorial Delegate to the 39th and 40th Congress: Politician, Extraordinary," *North Dakota History*. Vol. 33, No. 2 (Spring, 1966) 93-103.

Wilson, Wesley C. "General John B. S. Todd, First Delegate, Dakota Territory, Vol. 31, No. 3 (July, 1963) 189-194. *North Dakota History.*

Archives

Historical Resource Center, Pierre, South Dakota

Heritage Center, Bismarck, North Dakota

Chilson Room and South Dakota Manuscript Archives,
I. D. Weeks Library, University of South Dakota, Vermillion

Dakota Territorial Museum, Yankton, South Dakotas,
J.B.S. Todd Collection

Center for Western Studies,
Mikkelsen Library, Augustana College, Sioux Falls, SD

Newspapers of Dakota Territorial Days and of 1889-1890 Miscellaneous Files

Aberdeen American-News

Bismarck Tribune

Black Hills Daily Times

Black Hills Weekly Pioneer

Capital (Pierre)

Conklin's Dakotian (Watertown)

Dakota Democrat (Sioux Falls)

Dakota Herald (Yankton)

Dakota Journal (Pierre)
Deadwood Pioneer-Times
Fargo Forum
Grand Forks Herald
Huron Times
Jamestown Alert
Mitchell Daily Republican
Rapid City Journal
Sioux Falls Argus-Leader
Yankton Press
Yankton Press and Dakotian